SYMPHONY OF SEDUCTION

THE GREAT LOVE STORIES OF CLASSICAL COMPOSERS

CHRISTOPHER LAWRENCE

NERO

Thank you to Bradley Trevor Greive for suggesting the book's title.

Published by Nero,
an imprint of Schwartz Publishing Pty Ltd
Level 1, 221 Drummond Street
Carlton VIC 3053, Australia
enquiries@blackincbooks.com
www.blackincbooks.com

9781863958400 (paperback)
9781925435597 (ebook)

A catalogue record for this
book is available from the
National Library of Australia

Cover design by Peter Long and Marilyn de Castro
Text design and typesetting by Marilyn de Castro
Cover painting: 'Mars and Venus, Allegory of Peace'
by Louis Jean François Lagrenée

Printed by Sheridan in the United States of America

CONTENTS

INTRODUCTION

Classical music might not have claimed much of your attention in the past. You'd know if it had, because that's what it tries to do. There's a lot of organised thinking in there, reaching out with its notes, trying to hook you, draw you in, take you for a ride. *Very* elegantly, of course. Not a blunt proposition – more a wink across a crowded room. You must make your way through a host of misrepresentation, blind ignorance and bad publicity to reach this attractive stranger. Then the chat-up really begins.

It's not unreasonable to presume that those who thought up these intricate masterpieces of seduction would be just as good at the real thing. But, as I pointed out in my earlier book *Swooning*, the great composers were as inept at the business of what used to be called 'making love' as the rest of us. ('Inept' is too harsh a word, perhaps. Make that 'human'.)

This book examines that humanity in eleven stories about fabulously gifted people who venture out from their interior lives to find love. It might be the first time (Mozart), the final time (Berlioz), an inappropriate time (Debussy), a necessary time (Wagner), the only time (Satie), or the third time that week (Stradella). It might be something they want but can't have (Berlioz again), or something they *could* have but decide they don't want (Brahms). A couple of the stories are famous, but most of them are little more than vignettes. That's because almost every love story herein is unsuccessful; the two in this collection that carried through to a postscript did so for a comparatively short period, cut off by insanity, illness or death. 'Happily ever after' is *not* the take-away from these affairs of the heart. No oil sheik or tennis instructor in romantic fiction would be allowed such a failure rate. Truth is sometimes too disappointing, for all its strangeness.

And these *are* true stories – at least, in their timelines, people, locations, decisions. Many of the phrases are direct quotes from the composers themselves (my favourite is Puccini's 'I hate pavements'). On the other hand, coming up with the pillow talk that drives all of this was an entirely speculative endeavour, *ever* so much fun for this writer. In my own pleasant experience, while one's head is on the pillow, one's mind is often somewhere else.

When it came to primary sources, best of all was the music. The works of the great composers are the real engine of this book, featuring in and propelling the narrative, burbling away through every thought and every line of prose in a silent soundtrack. Individual works are the starting point of the stories in several cases; the Mozart and Stradella chapters even begin with a description of the act of composition. While writing, I used these works to colour in my outlines of their creators, and it's my most fervent hope that reading this book will inspire you to do the same. Every piece referred to in these

$\mathcal{S}$YMPHONY
OF $\mathcal{S}$EDUCTION

Christopher Lawrence is one of Australia's favourite radio
personalities through his work on ABC Classic FM. As a recording
producer, Christopher has received an International Emmy for
Performing Arts, three ARIAs and the Editors' Choice Award at
the Cannes Classical Awards. He has conducted most of Australia's
capital city symphony orchestras and is the author of three
previous books.

pages can be easily sourced. If that seems like too specialised a task, a *Symphony of Seduction* soundtrack is available on CD or to download. Listen as you read; you'll find the sounds of these composers to be a poignant counterpoint to the tales of their stuttering dreams. Therein lie the *real* truths of these lives – and ours. For when it comes to putting a little love into your day, classical music does the best job of all.

— *Christopher Lawrence*

A PEAR-SHAPED AFFAIR

A classic story of love among the bohemians in
the Montmartre area of Paris: he, the eccentric café
pianist who became one of music's greatest originals;
she, a former artist's model who featured in the
paintings of Renoir. The flame burned bright for
only a short time in such a milieu – but could he
have been jealous enough to murder her?

~

*'When I was young, people used to say to me "Wait until you're fifty,
you'll see". I am fifty. I haven't seen anything.'*

Erik Satie (1866–1925)

In his squalid apartment in 1916, Erik Satie peers at the mirror through pince-nez to inspect his attire for the morning's
journey into Paris, as if noticing something for the first time.

'This strikes me as entirely familiar,' he says to himself.
'Could it be that I was wearing the same thing yesterday?'

Then, chuckling at his regular private joke, he responds, 'Of course I was.'

He looks exactly the same every day, for his wardrobe contains only six identical suits. In this current phase of his fashion life he presents as a civil servant: bowler hat, dark jacket, a stiff shirt collar (he has 144 ready to wear) and, always, an umbrella. He also carries a hammer – just in case.

Fifteen years earlier he dressed exclusively in velvet, and before that, when he was the founder and only member of his own church, he strolled around Paris in something resembling a cassock.

The long, lank hair of his youth is now combed onto the back of his head from a line near the crown, and a goatee bristles from his chin like a tongue of flame. Even if his eyes don't carbonise the object of their gaze like those of his friend Picasso, they have a sufficiently quizzical expression to cause the more observant passer-by to doubt the complacency of this apparent paragon of the bourgeoisie.

Erik wants his appearance to deceive. He wants to portray himself as worldly, even though there has never been a composer so resolutely extraterrestrial. Beneath the surface of modest affluence there is only poverty, his most constant companion, 'a sad little girl with large green eyes' who dictates his moods, his work and his choice of residence away from even the cheapest Parisian garret. For him, poverty is a more poetic state than destitution, which he describes as 'that woman with the huge breasts'.

The sad little girl has brought him to a backwater called Arcueil, where he has taken lodgings in what is known locally as 'The House of Four Chimneys', a structure compressed into a wedge by the acute confluence of two streets. He eventually lives in that same room for twenty-seven years. In all that time, nobody else ever sets foot in it.

Erik is a recluse, perhaps, but only when his door is closed. Once he arrives in Paris, he becomes a man about town, with meetings in bars and cafés over an apéritif – or ten. 'It's odd,' he says. 'You find people in every bar willing to offer you a drink. No one ever dreams of presenting you with a sandwich.'

It is time for his morning pilgrimage: the ten kilometres from his room into town. Well after midnight, he will walk all the way home again, stopping on occasion under a streetlamp to retrieve his notebook and scribble down a musical idea.

Prior to leaving, Erik receives the first mail from the concierge, one of six that will arrive that day. It includes what is obviously a bill from yet another mercenary utilities provider. Without bothering to check the contents, he places the offending document inside the topmost of two grand pianos stacked upside down upon the other, where it will vanish under a patina of dust like its unopened predecessors.

Emerging onto the street, he walks slowly, taking small steps, stopping at regular haunts along the way to fortify himself for the next stage of the journey. At Chez Tulard he is greeted like the town councillor he once aspired to be.

'Something extra in your *café*, monsieur?' says the owner, indicating the cognac.

'*D'accord*,' says Satie.

Two kilometres further on, he feels a rush of inspiration and pauses at the bar of Monsieur Aknine to anticipate the notes that may come forth.

'An absinthe, Monsieur Satie?' comes the ritual question.

In another favourite stop, now with Paris in sight, a curious regular asks Satie if his profession is truly that of a composer. 'Everyone will tell you that I am not a musician,' says Satie. 'That is true. Don't imagine that my work is music. That's not my line.'

'Another kir, monsieur?' ventures the waiter.

'Such is inevitable,' says the alleged non-musician, dabbing at his lips with one of ninety-nine freshly laundered handkerchiefs.

While the streetscape along the way has altered considerably over the decades (shop windows displaying the new *haute couture*, Metro stops sprouting from the ground, horse-drawn carriages giving way to automobiles) it has happened in such tiny increments as to be unnoticeable to the daily walker. Blind to his surroundings, even with quizzical eyes, the now flushed civil servant is instead preoccupied this morning by music – and the memories that come with it.

His implacable walk is just like the stride of the left hand pivoting up and down the piano keyboard in his *Gnossienne No. 5*, one of those pieces he wrote more than twenty years ago, just before he fell in love. Above these musical footsteps, the right hand meanders through a tune that never develops or resolves, requoting itself in an attempt to loop back to the beginning; tipsy, yet maintaining its elegance. Like Erik, really.

What did that title mean? Something old and Greek, he recalled, a description casting the work out of time, beyond bar lines and time signatures and all the bondage that institutional music came to demand of her creators when she turned into a dominatrix.

That was the trouble with memory; it kept reintroducing one to people it would have been far better to avoid. Erik pauses at his reflection in a window to make sure the brim of his hat is exactly level above his eyes. If the fifth *Gnossienne* is just like him, it has to be admitted that the others in the set are very much like *her*. They are cat music: the first *Gnossienne* brushes your ankles as it passes by, and the fourth purrs in your lap while the kneading of extended claws reminds you who is in charge.

Suzanne was a cat – or a sphinx. She always landed on her feet, even when pushed from a third-floor window, due in no small part to her early training as a trapeze artist. The similarity of the music and the person was of course a coincidence, because the first *Gnossienne* had been composed before Erik and Suzanne ever met. But she was already somewhere nearby – just next door, in fact – when those notes went on the page back in the last century. Somehow, without yet knowing her, he must have been aware that a storm was coming. Artists are like ants when it comes to anticipating bad weather, pointing their antennae in its direction and rushing for the nearest hole.

~

It was New Year's Eve at the Auberge du Clou in Montmartre and another round of drinks had been served as the assembled bohemians waited in the small room for 1893 to begin. The cellar was dark except for the lamps at the bar, the glowing tips of cigarettes, and the rectangle of light on the wall where a shadow-puppet play had just been performed with piano interludes from a young man wearing a top hat, Windsor tie and long frock coat, a black ribbon dangling from his pince-nez.

His duties as house musician over for a while, Erik was nursing an absinthe in the corner when a woman from a table of what sounded like painter types approached him. This was an almost unprecedented occurrence, as he was renowned for having no money. Her presence made him nervous. He wondered if there was a hole nearby darker than the one they were in.

'Thank you for the music tonight, monsieur,' she said. 'My friends and I especially liked that slow one; the one like a waltz.'

'And merci to you, mademoiselle,' he said. 'You must be referring to my third *Gymnopédie*. Your friends are perceptive. It is a work that has been publicly acclaimed as a marvel.'

'Gymnopédie?' she asked. 'I've not heard the word. What does it mean?'

'Something old and Greek. The word is my own invention.'

'Whatever it's called, it's beautiful.'

So are you, thought Erik, even though in the dim light he could see little more than feline eyes and the centre parting in a thick helmet of hair. 'Beautiful as it is, the music's real value is therapeutic,' he said. 'It has cured a man who suffered for eight years with a liver disorder, rheumatic pains and polyps on the nose.'

Her eyes narrowed and her tone became more playful. 'That is indeed *formidable*. How do you know this to be true?'

'It was in our cabaret magazine, *The Japanese Divan*,' he said. 'I read this claim in print only days after I wrote it. These days, artists cannot merely create their work; they must make a place where their work can flourish. Exotic fruit needs a conservatory in this Parisian weather.' He wondered if she lived in a conservatory.

'If that was your third *Gymnopédie*, there must be at least a couple of others,' she said. 'If I come back another time, might you play them for me?'

'I will play them until all of your polyps have disappeared,' he said with a flourish he hoped displayed more wit than accusation. As she turned away to give him a momentary glimpse of her profile he could see from the smooth line of her nose that no musical therapy was necessary, while the curve of her lower back near the hip indicated a flexibility that could only exist without a trace of rheumatism. The empty bottles on the table at which she rejoined her companions were a reminder that Erik could not presume anything about her liver.

~

'Erik with a *k*?' she asked a few nights later, peering at his hand-drawn card. This time she had come alone and was waiting at his table when he had finished applying musical therapy around the room.

'I was born with a *c*, but changed it as soon as I could,' he explained. 'Those of us from Normandy consider ourselves little Vikings. A *k* is more Scandinavian.'

'Which side of your family is Scandinavian?'

This was harder for Erik to answer, because his mother had been half-Scot. Not only was he more authentically an Eric, he should probably have been playing the piano in a kilt.

It was only their second conversation, yet already Erik's stream of invention was beginning to run dry, probably because in his twenty-six years he had never had two successive conversations with *any* woman except his paternal grandmother.

At this rate he was going to have to resort to the truth about himself, and that had always been calamitous for him in the past, for there was nothing about which he could boast. Derided and expelled from the Paris Conservatoire, sharing clothes with friends through mutual lack of funds, and already fretting about his thinning hair, he could not provide an assurance of becoming prosperous or attractive at any point during the next six months. The rest of his life looked equally dubious.

But still they talked, and Erik began to realise that such shortcomings were of no concern to her, for Suzanne Valadon was not of the bourgeoisie. He also learned the reason for the exquisite shape of her back.

'A trapeze artist!' he repeated, his imagination leaping from *Gymnopédies* to gymnastics.

'A long time ago,' she said. 'But eventually I was drawn away from the highwire towards High Art.'

Being a toned and supple seventeen-year-old girl had meant that entrée into the milieu of painters entailed taking her clothes off. Suzanne modelled for people like Renoir and Toulouse-Lautrec. Another painter and creator of shadow-puppet plays, Miguel Utrillo, was considered the most likely in a wide field to have fathered her now ten-year-old son, Maurice. Clearly, modelling was a risky business.

Those days were over, and Suzanne was now an artist in her own right with an atelier next to Erik's on the rue Cortot. He remembered that he had seen her before, always in a retinue of painters, some of them mutual friends. All the poor artists lived in Montmartre until the bourgeoisie, who came to believe it would be fashionable to live near poor artists, ousted them.

'And since I have had the honour to hear some of your work, perhaps you would like to come and see some of mine?' she said. 'Unless, of course, you would prefer we go to your place.'

Satie's throat suddenly tightened so much that his next gulp of *vin de table* was stopped in its tracks. Even though Montmartre was a small world, his world was even smaller.

'My place presents a slight problem,' he said. 'A problem of dimension.'

'I have been in small rooms before,' she purred.

'This is *very* small,' he continued, not bothering to conceal his embarrassment. 'I call it The Cupboard. There is no room for anything but a bed, so it also has to serve as my work table, my wardrobe and my filing cabinet.'

'How quaint! Is it also your playground?' she said, unaware that the tease was lost in his veil of panic.

'In any event, Suzanne, the issue is not so much that of *width*. It has more to do with *height*. Once inside my door, it is impossible to stand up.' This was an attempt to reclassify a hovel as an architectural misjudgement.

'Erik, it *is* possible that we won't stand up for the rest of the evening,' she said, incredulous at his naiveté. 'So come with me. It is *my* walls that I want you to see after all, and you may find my ceiling is far enough from the floor to suit your purpose.'

Just as Suzanne had promised, the ceiling in her third-floor apartment was beyond his reach, and the rooms spacious enough for the frock coat she slid from his shoulders to lie on the floor without being in anyone's way. There was more light here than the fashionable gloom of the Clou, enough for Erik to appreciate the artwork on the walls. One of them, a painting of

Suzanne and her former partner by the Catalan painter Santiago Rusiñol, gave him a shock of recognition. Two years before, Utrillo had borrowed Satie's old infantryman's uniform to wear for a sitting, and there it was in a portrait hanging on her wall.

'You see, Erik?' she said, pouring out wine. 'You've been here before.'

There was also a self-portrait Suzanne had made ten years before that he could compare to the real thing, now that her face was finally more fully revealed by the generous lamplight. It was fascinating to see somebody in the past and the present for the first time. Her line with the crayon on paper was already assured, and the expression she captured was the wary arrogance of a teenager. A decade later, there was no trace of it as she clinked her glass against his. The wide-spaced blue eyes were more appraising, the generous lips more succulent than petulant.

'Do you appreciate my skill as much as I appreciate yours?' she asked.

'I do. But your art says more about you than mine about me.'

'You're wrong. My images are just an approximation, but your music describes you completely. To hear it is to know you. That is why you are here. There is nothing more you need to say.'

Erik was unused to such compliments, and felt his mask slipping. 'My *Gymnopédies* are absurd. They are simple crap. And they are short.'

'Voilà. Simple, short, crap? That's life. Do you want to see my older skills? I still have them.'

'Such as?' he said, his voice cracking slightly.

'You know I was an acrobat in the circus? It was fun, because

I was poor and it took me away from the boring life of selling hats and vegetables and carrying plates of food to ungrateful people. When you are fifteen, your body can do almost anything you want. But you have to do it perfectly every time, or else there are bad mistakes. One day I fell from the trapeze . . .'

'*Mon Dieu!*' cried Satie, in a brief reprise of a previous spiritual phase.

'Nothing serious, but enough to tell me that my time as an acrobat was over,' she said. 'That was more than ten years ago. It's funny. There are some things the body never forgets – at least, not yet. Sit on my bed, and I will show you. And please, take off your hat.'

Satie suspected that this would be unlike any circus routine he had ever seen, but did as he was told while assessing the suitability of Suzanne's body for the announced performance. Rather than the gaunt figure of a hungry *bohémienne*, hers was voluptuous enough to make any Impressionist reach hungrily for the brush.

'Strength and flexibility are paramount. Witness.' At this, she bent herself back at the waist until her extended hands touched the floor behind her.

'Handstand.'

First one leg, and then the other were kicked upward to point at the ceiling. Her wrists became her ankles, and her ankles were very much on display as her dress inverted completely and fell to the floor, covering her head and exposing her knickers. Here at last was a part of Suzanne yet to be committed to canvas. He wished he could have played it on the piano. One day, he would try. He could hear a waltz.

She swung her legs over to complete the circle and straightened up.

'Now we will have a little trapeze,' she announced.

Erik looked upwards, half-expecting a fly bar to swing from the top of her small armoire.

'I am the flyer, you are the catcher, and we will attempt a shooting star. I will approach with my legs apart, and then you take my hands. Ready? Hup-hup!'

He felt that somehow he wasn't ready – but what could he do? The circus had come to town.

She launched herself and became airborne after two or three bounds, lifting and separating her legs until they were parallel with her arms. He was aware of a forest of limbs hurtling towards him like javelins. When their bodies collided he was knocked backwards into a prone position on the bed while she straddled him from above, her legs still fully extended on either side. Strangely, he was more winded than she was.

She lowered herself to his side so that they were lying face to face.

'That could have been fatal,' she said with mock reproach. 'You didn't catch me. Now I am just a falling star.'

He grasped the copper-red hair that Renoir had painted.

'My beautiful supple chérie,' he said in a voice he did not recognise. 'It is I who am falling.'

'In that case, we had better remove your pince-nez before you land on something hard,' she said.

So it was she who caught him, demonstrating that her body had indeed forgotten nothing, and that a reverse somersault was not required for her to execute the arch in her back.

'I will never forget that this was Saturday, January four-teenth,' he said immediately afterwards. 'It is the day I proposed to you.'

She was confused. 'Are you talking to me or making a diary entry, *mon petit?*'

'Both,' he said. 'I want you to marry me. We should be together for the rest of our lives, because I do not think I will fall in love again.'

He began to hum a waltz tune, and then added words that had obviously been in his head long before this night:

We are far from moderation
And further yet from sadness
I long only for the precious moment
When we will be happy
I want you.

She was too transfixed by the melody and the absurdity of his impulse to refuse him then and there. Not until he slept did she whisper the sensible answer into his ear, hoping it would make its way into the place in his head where he kept all those poignant aimless tunes, to spill out between the notes when he was next at the keyboard in the Clou. It would not be the answer he wanted, but the susurration made him smile.

~

Two days later Suzanne came to see him in The Cupboard next door, ensuring her head never touched his low ceiling, and it was then their affair truly began. Each night she would wait at his table at the Clou until he had played the popular ballads, or accompanied another Utrillo puppet creation. Suzanne's former suitor had noticed that Satie was the latest object of her attentions. He seemed not to mind.

Her enthusiasm for Erik's music made him more ambitious. He composed a ballet about the conversion of a pagan to Christianity that was eventually staged at the Clou with a large cast of puppets. Satie presided at a harmonium, an instrument he thought more mystical in sound; the audience reacted by either shouting him a drink or shouting abuse. This was enough for the work to be offered to the Paris Opéra. When its director failed to respond in time, Satie challenged him to a duel. Excerpts from the work were published privately in a deluxe edition with Suzanne's cover design featuring her lover in profile.

He inscribed music to her with sketches of the new bob in her hair, and she paid him the supreme compliment of painting his portrait, saving her brightest colours for his red cheeks and eyes bluer than her own. He made her portrait in return, but while she gave him hers, he decided to keep her likeness for himself. It was the only way she could be with him all the time.

Too soon, within weeks, she was not at the Clou every night, and when he asked Utrillo where she might be the answers were too vague for comfort. Erik sat in his room by day, planning appointments and writing invitations to her on notepaper upon which he had inscribed a chicken as the coat of arms.

'Dear little Biqui,' he wrote. 'Impossible to stop thinking about your whole being. You are in Me complete.' Erik took another sip, being careful not to drink so much that the precision of his calligraphy would be spoiled, but enough to burst into self-pitying tears. 'For Me there is only the icy solitude that fills my heart with sorrow.' Could he not see her somehow? Could she not make herself available '1. This evening at 8.45 at my place; 2. Tomorrow morning again at my place; 3. Tomorrow evening ...'

'Erik, you must try to stop being so abject,' she said several nights later, when they finally met again. 'I have my work and my other friends.'

'I am becoming terribly reasonable,' he said, desperate to hide the intensity of his feelings under a mantle of noble resignation. 'In spite of the happiness it gives me to see you, I am beginning to understand that you can't always do what you want.'

'You don't know me as well as you think, Erik. I've been other people's servant, their plaything, for too long. Now, I *always* do what I want. Our liaison gives me pleasure for now, but I don't want it every day.'

'Then I shall begin to understand that instead,' he said. 'You see, Biqui? There is a beginning to everything.'

'This is not the beginning,' she said.

～

'How can this be the end?' he sobbed.

It was three months later, during which time he had written letters daily, as much to himself as to her. He had found their maudlin tone so naked, so shocking, so *unlike* him that he resolved never to send them. They would only have elicited her pity.

The tree in the rear courtyard of Suzanne's building was an

explosion of green, and warm air drifted in through the open window where she stood. Summer had arrived in Montmartre, but while the neighbourhood was coming to life, something on the third floor of a building was dying.

'There is someone else,' she said, her voice more level than his.

'We were together at my place only three nights ago!' he said. 'On Saturday. It was wonderful. Saturday is our weekly anniversary.'

'I wanted you to have a happy anniversary. It is my fare-well gift.'

'Does this person know that you are gifting yourself around the neighbourhood?'

'He understands me better than you do. Now he would like something more.'

Satie abruptly pushed his pince-nez back into position. 'I offered you something more the first time I came here. You declined me, yet you are prepared to give him whatever he expects. What does he do?'

'He is a banker,' she said.

A *banker*? Erik could not believe it. He had spent five months beginning to understand Suzanne as someone totally immune to the corruption of commitment and the other trappings of an upper-class existence. 'Fuck the rich,' she used to say, echoing the artist's mantra. Now she had.

His cheeks became redder than the ones in her painting.

'Suzanne, you have taken all of me. I cannot let you get away with this,' he cried, rushing at her.

~

'You're joking! Out the window?' said an incredulous Picasso in a Paris café, twenty-three years later. The two were sharing a table with Jean Cocteau.

'You can imagine how bad I felt after I pushed her,' replied Satie, still recovering from the exertion of his daily walk from Arcueil. 'It was three floors up above a paved courtyard.'

'What did you do?' asked Cocteau.

'What any man of honour would have done: I left her apartment straight away, reported to the nearest police station, and turned myself in for having murdered my girlfriend. I was careful to explain it was a crime of passion.'

'That is the best crime one can commit,' said the Spaniard. 'And then?'

'I accompanied the police back to the rue Cortot where we searched for Suzanne's body in the courtyard. That is when things became more complicated.'

'What do you mean?'

'The body wasn't there.'

'Suzanne had disappeared? But how can this be?'

'You know she was a circus acrobat in early life? The police decided she must have performed a triple pike on the way down, landed on her feet, and walked away.'

'From a three-storey fall? Impossible!' said Cocteau.

'Erik, are you sure you pushed her?' said the painter, with a smirk.

'No,' Satie admitted.

The trio ordered another round of Ricards to contemplate this miracle.

'So, what do you think about love these days?' asked Cocteau, retrieving his notebook.

'I have avoided it ever since. Right afterwards, I considered it a sickness of the nerves. Look how sentimental Debussy has been about it! He used to be very good to me – those orchestrations he made of the first and third *Gymnopédies* pulled me out of a hole – until that love life of his made a mess of things. On the other hand, I am slightly more sentimental about love than, say, Ravel. Who knows what *he* has ever had to do with it? I find it very comical.'

'I think it is time for another wine,' said Picasso. 'We have our ballet project *Parade* to discuss. Unless, of course, you would rather have a sandwich.'

'A sandwich!' said Satie, horrified. 'Never touch the stuff.'

POSTSCRIPT

When Erik Satie died from cirrhosis of the liver in 1925 at the age of fifty-nine, he left behind a corpus of work that included titles such as *Desiccated Embryos*, *Drivelling Preludes for a Dog*, *The Angora Ox*, *Unpleasant Glimpses*, the *Three Pieces in the Shape of a Pear*, and a song heavily indebted to his cabaret and music-hall days called 'I Want You' ('*Je te veux*').

He also left the contents of a rented apartment in the Parisian suburb of Arcueil that none of his friends had ever seen. When they entered the unknown inner sanctum they found a bed, a table and chair, newspapers, old hats, walking sticks, umbrellas and two pianos stuffed with papers that included two major musical compositions Satie thought he had left on a bus.

Deeper below the dust they found a bundle of letters that had obviously never been sent to Suzanne Valadon, who by now had married and divorced her banker, only to take up with a man twenty-two years her junior.

The late composer's brother, Conrad, offered to deliver the sacred cache to its intended recipient. Erik would have no cause to be embarrassed by the contents now; he had new cafés to visit and perhaps even a deity to offend. At the burial vault, Conrad could swear he heard his brother's voice saying to God: 'Just give me time to put on a petticoat, and then I'm yours.'

Suzanne was clearly moved by the offer. She would have been made aware by mutual acquaintances and gossip that she had never been replaced in his life, and that their portraits had hung side by side in his apartment on otherwise bare walls for more than a quarter of a century. She wrote in reply that 'so many memories are heart-rending indeed and yet very sweet to me'. Without realising, she signed her name twice.

The letters were duly placed in her care. Suzanne set aside several days to read and re-read them, being taken back to the Montmartre of 1893 and the story of two young, independent artists who found each other for less than half a year. With each letter she paused to let the memories follow: the sound of a piano playing, a man's voice singing 'I want you' on a winter's night.

She slowly placed each letter on coloured paper back in its envelope, making sure to preserve the integrity of the original folds.

Then she burned them.

Love Makes War

Robert Schumann was the archetypal Romantic composer, and the young, beautiful Clara Wieck one of the most celebrated piano virtuosos in Europe. All they wanted was to make beautiful music together, but there was one huge obstacle to overcome: her father. The battle for Clara, escalating from subterfuge and forced separations to public slander and legal action, was as brutal and protracted as any war.

~

'There is no more powerful stimulus to imagination than tensions and longing for something.'

Robert Schumann (1810–1856)

It was when they arrived at the bottom of the stairs, where the glow of the lamp she was holding cast a sheen over the front door, that Robert decided Clara just had to be kissed.

The thought had been with him for some time, and now that she was sixteen it seemed as good a time as any.

She lifted the latch and was turning to wish him goodnight when he slid his arm around her waist and drew her towards him slowly enough to give her time to pull away. Instead, she came willingly to his mouth with all the resolution of a perfect cadence.

They kissed lightly at first, and then more hungrily as she followed his example with the precocity of a quick study. Robert remembered Romeo's instruction to 'let lips do what hands do' and thought it was bad luck for the young Veronese that Juliet was not a virtuoso pianist. Clara's mouth progressed from simple scales to arpeggios in no time at all, and as she moved to the cadenza her eyelids fluttered. The kiss settled into a clear A major final chord before a slow release of lips into post-performance silence. He half-expected the sound of applause.

There was still light around them, and he realised she had held the lamp aloft all the while with the self-possession of a seasoned performer.

'Darkness all around, yet our first kiss bathed in light,' he said, always looking for the most poetic spin.

'Was it?' she replied. 'Everything went dark from where I was standing. I thought I was going to faint. Who did I kiss just now – Florestan, or Eusebius?' She was referring to the names he had long since given to the opposing sides of his nature.

'You kissed Robert the composer, who adores you,' he said. 'Chiarina, my music has known about this for a long time without telling the person who created it. And now *I* know.' It felt right to say it, not as a confession, but as a summation of all the years of half-knowing.

'We can't talk now,' she said. 'It is late. I am showing you out. This is my father's house.' She was aware of how little time was left before Wieck would come looking for her.

'So it begins,' he said, stepping out over the threshold. He was hot and trembling despite being her elder by some nine years with experience in matters such as this, while Clara's hands were steady and her brow dry after her near swoon. The cold November air would be a tonic. He had to consider what should come after a kiss on the stairs.

~

The gusting autumn leaves in Leipzig's cobbled streets matched the commotion of Schumann's thoughts. There were the after-shocks of that kiss. Clara had been a part of his life ever since her childhood; what had just happened redefined them both. He would try to diminish its sensuality if he could, and instead dwell on the poetry of the moment. As always with Robert, with poetry came the music.

His mind surged with the notes he had put to paper that afternoon. *Carnaval* was about a gallery of people he loved and admired, mingling at a fantastical masked ball with an unruly troupe of commedia dell'arte characters. His own Florestan and Eusebius rubbed shoulders with Pierrot and Harlequin; Clara was there in a minor-key waltz called *Chiarina*. Next to her was Chopin, about whom Robert had declared in an ecstatic review: 'Hats off, gentlemen! A genius!' He wondered if the day would come when someone might say that about himself.

Time wasn't exactly on his side if he was going to do some-thing remarkable with his life. First he had been going to be a lawyer, if only to please his mother. Then he was going to be a pianist, until the homemade gadget he contrived from a cigar box to make his fingers stronger had precisely the opposite effect. It yanked one finger at a time back towards the wrist while the others were in use, but when he released the middle finger of his right hand after a strenuous practice session he discovered the bloody thing wouldn't work any more.

Short-lived as this ambition proved to be, it at least had led him to Clara. She was only eight when they met, when her father, Friedrich, agreed to teach piano to the teenage university law student. Even then her precocity at the piano was extraordinary. She was already preparing for her first major concert appearance while Robert morosely picked away at his scales, smoking one cigar after another.

With the child Clara he felt complicity based on a shared love of music. They pored over scores together and took long walks, during which she teased him by tugging the back of his coat, her laughter tinkling in the air.

She was about to begin her first major European tour at thirteen when she met Schumann's mother, who playfully (and perhaps intuitively) joked that someday Clara should marry 'my Robert'. Clara blushed, but Robert didn't see it quite that way. They were not a boyfriend and girlfriend, he declared, or even a brother and sister: he was a 'pilgrim', and she the 'distant shrine'.

Meanwhile, the pilgrim made regular visits to another place of worship between the legs of Christel, who couldn't play the piano at all. Her appetite for sex was exceeded only by Robert's capacity for post-coital guilt. Since he visited her several times a week, he felt guilty much of the time, and catching syphilis from the damned woman didn't help. At least he had taken the arsenic cure as soon as he noticed the sores, and both they and, presumably, the disease, had cleared. If only he could also eradicate his desires! They tainted what should have been the pure nature of the great creative artist.

'I am sinking back into the old slime!' he lamented. 'Will no hand come from the clouds to hold me back? *I* must become that hand!'

'Oh Robbie, such theatrics,' Christel replied with a half-lidded gaze over the rim of her naked breast. 'Let *me* give you a hand.' Then she grasped the architect of his despair.

There was *that* night – he remembered it was during October in 1833 – when he thought he was losing his mind, just like some of the poets he admired. Loneliness and a pervading sense of failure froze him into something 'hardly more than a statue'. Standing at his fourth-floor window and watching the shattered moonlight on the stones of the courtyard below, he resolved to kill himself. Somehow he made it through to the morning. Soon after, he visited a doctor, hoping there might be some remedy.

'Medicine won't be any help to you, Herr Schumann. You need to find yourself a wife. She will soon cure you.'

The music of *Carnaval* fell back into his mind, and the next piece in the sequence after the homage to Chopin: *Estrella*, his poetic nickname for Ernestine, another of Wieck's piano students. Oh God, what was he going to do?

Taking the doctor's advice, he had quickly developed what he thought to be a romance with Ernestine. He saw her as delicate, while she was attracted to the way he pursed his lips, his thoughtful silences and the way his brown hair tumbled over his forehead. Her father was a baron, her mother a countess, and there was little chance they would countenance their daughter living in a composer's garret – meaning that superior accommodation might be provided.

Robert didn't behave with Ernestine the way he did with Christel. Instead, they gazed at each other significantly, spoke of the moral purity of every great creative artist and refrained from even holding each other's hand. He dedicated an allegro to her. The platonic lovers were soon engaged, and it seemed as if all Robert's problems and temptations were conquered. He even moved to lodgings on the ground floor.

But then Ernestine proved not to be as aristocratic as he thought. A year after their engagement, he discovered she was not the daughter of a baron. Instead, she was the illegitimate progeny of a baron's wife's sister and a man unknown; probably the redheaded stablehand with the nice thighs. Robert could hold Ernestine's hand as passionately as he liked, but he would never find any gold coins clasped in it.

Meanwhile, Clara returned from yet another European tour in the company of her svengali father. She had changed into a woman of the world, a true sophisticate, and she looked at him in a different way.

Her shrine was no longer distant.

The music in Robert's head stopped. Now he sensed only the cold as the night of an approaching winter closed in. Shivering, he clasped the thick collar of his coat. His body heat was drained like fuel by the process of recollection. All that remained was the imprint of warmth on his lips. That kiss . . .

This much was clear: he must break with Ernestine. What he

had said to Clara on her father's doorstep was true. Something *had* begun. He and Clara were perfectly suited to one another, were destined to be together, and would inspire each other. She would be the supreme interpreter of all the great music that he would now compose for her. In her hands, the qualities in his works that many had found inscrutable – brevity, formlessness, secret codes, literary allusions – would make perfect sense. And no one would be more delighted by this outcome than Clara's father, who had made it his sole purpose to prepare his gifted daughter for a life in the service of Art.

The street had grown quiet now, excepting the distant murmur of a corner tavern where Robert intended to go for a beer to massage his thoughts. It was easy to distinguish the footsteps that approached him rapidly from behind.

Somebody is in as much of a hurry to get to that tavern as I am, he thought.

'Schumann!' A hand grasped his shoulder, spinning him around.

He looked into the red face of Friedrich Wieck, breathless from the pursuit. His glaring eyes made an odd contrast to his otherwise insipid features and the foppish cut of his hair that now lay in damp strands across his forehead.

'Herr Wieck, I feel there is something I should speak with you about . . .' began Schumann.

'I know what is going on!' whispered Wieck, exhaling huge clouds of mist in the air. 'You and *my Clara*!'

'*That's* what we must discuss —' said Schumann, attempting to continue his first interrupted sentence.

'We will discuss *nothing*!' said Wieck, again cutting him off.

He stepped forward and seized the front of Schumann's coat. Robert recalled seeing Wieck doing the same with Clara's brother Alwin when he'd played badly in one of his father's piano lessons. That time, the boy had been thrown to the floor.

'I will make this simple so that you understand, Herr Schumann,' Wieck said slowly, his mouth snarling inches from Robert's face. 'If I see you in my house again, if I see you *anywhere* attempting to speak to my daughter – I will shoot you.'

Wieck pushed Robert away and turned in the direction of his house, where a sobbing Clara waited behind a locked bedroom door. Schumann watched the retreating figure and then turned in the direction of the tavern, walking now with more speed than before.

～

'He's not going to shoot you,' said Clara, stroking his hair, teasing it around her tapered fingers. 'He would lose everything: his reputation, me, and the money I will make.'

It was three months later, and the couple were in Dresden. Clara had gone there with her father, who had then to return to Leipzig unexpectedly on business. Robert seized the opportunity to enjoy Clara's lips for three days by making his pilgrimage to the neighbouring city. Unchaperoned as they were, Clara was not Christel, and her shrine remained unsullied.

He had severed his engagement with Ernestine, each returning their ring to the other. She showed more maturity and understanding than he could see in himself. 'I always thought you could only love Clara,' she said.

Robert cupped Clara's face with his good hand. 'I'm beginning to feel that your father would do it just for the satisfaction of knowing you'd be tainted goods,' he said. 'If he can't have you, nobody can.'

'He's behaving like a feudal lord because I'm not yet of age,' she said, 'but he's a lord trying to control a revolution; a revolution called Love. Music is my life, and since you *are* music, then you will become my life. The best my father can do is try to keep us apart – and he hasn't done very well at it *this* time.'

~

Robert did not see or speak with her again for another eighteen months.

Clara's father learned of the clandestine liaison in Dresden and had turned the Leipzig house into a fortress. Schumann was officially expunged from her past by Wieck's insistence that she return all of the composer's letters while asking him in turn to return hers.

Robert sought his familiar consolations: drink, and the accepting warmth of Christel. She had given him the pox years before and could hardly infect him again. This time her embraces were without risk.

'*Pregnant?*' he said, incredulous.

'If you bob into the barrel enough times, my love, you eventually get an apple,' she said.

A daughter was born early the following year. 'Consequences,' he noted in his diary. That was all.

His landlady had another nasty surprise.

'*Out?*' he repeated, again incredulous.

'I'm sorry, Herr Schumann,' she said. 'I've been very fond of you for a long time, but I won't tolerate your behaviour any longer. The other tenants are complaining about the noise you make with your friends, and it's not proper for those women to keep coming and going at all hours. This is a *respectable* house.'

His music was going nowhere. Publishers were turning a cold shoulder. There were few performances with even fewer reviews. And yet the further he tried to push Clara's face from his mind, the more music came rushing in.

His landlady let him stay, and his days became a frenzy of scribbling as hundreds of pages began to mount up on his piano lid. He had felt enslaved at times by indulging his desires; now, to want and not to have was liberating at least a part of him: the part of greatest originality.

The public wanted the glamour and tinsel of Liszt and Paganini, the cascades of notes, the bravado, the circus tricks of virtuosity. The academics wanted a seriousness of purpose that came with large forms, elaborate structures, cities of sound.

Schumann knew that neither was his way. His first attempt at a symphony had been a disaster. In speech, just as on manuscript paper, he was not a gusher; prolixity had no place in his musical lexicon. Since ideas sped by in his mind he felt their expression should be equally swift. He knew that such discretion was not the fashion, but hoped the public would eventually come to prefer the whispered aside to the endless peroration. Nothing said more than a succinct 'I love you'.

He kept that in mind while composing *Träumerei* (or *Dreaming*) in his *Scenes from Childhood*, inspired by Clara's observation that at times he seemed like a child; not infantile, but simple in his response to things. All of his music was for her, full of things that would pass by unnoticed in a concert hall. He knew it would bring her to tears if they could only exchange it with each other away from the world.

One day an intermediary arrived with requests from Clara: could she have back his letters to her? And would he come in a couple of days to a concert in which she was playing some of his *Symphonic Etudes*?

He went, she played, and the world exploded. He asked the question.

'One *yes* is all you want, my darling?' she said. 'What an important little word it is! I can indeed say it. *Yes*. My inmost soul whispers it to you.'

'You will be of age in a few weeks,' said Robert. 'On that day I can and I will ask your father for your hand.'

'Surely God won't turn my eighteenth birthday into a day of trouble? He couldn't be that cruel,' said Clara.

~

'My life is torn up at the roots,' said Robert. 'The interview with your father was terrible. His is a new way to kill. He drives in the hilt as well as the blade.'

Schumann looked exhausted when they met secretly in the house of one of his friends. After spending so much time alone in thought, he seemed to have physically disappeared into himself, eyes sinking beneath a puffy face. Even his hair was lifeless, pasted onto his head like an ill-fitting toupée.

'I expected to confront a volcano, and instead found a glacier,' he continued. 'He was cold – *cold*. His answer was a perplexing mixture of refusal and consent, a path of torture to the altar without dismissing the idea of marriage completely. We're to wait two more years, meet only in public during that time, and have no correspondence unless you are travelling. In the meantime, I am to amass a fortune big enough for you to be kept in the manner in which he feels you should be accustomed. Oh yes – he would also like me to fly to the moon. He wants to auction you off to the highest bidder, like any good businessman. He actually said to me, "Hearts? What do I care about *hearts?*"'

'It's the money he's worried about, Robert. You admit that your brothers are still extending loans to help you get by. My father thinks you won't be able to support me. If marriage curtails my career *I* won't be able to support us either. He didn't raise me to be a hausfrau. I have promised him to pursue my art for some years yet. It's what I also want for myself. Next month my father and I are leaving for a tour to Vienna. We could be away for a while.'

'How long is a while?'

'Seven months.'

'Seven *months*? We've only just seen each other again after being apart for *eighteen* months! We're doomed to spend our best years apart! How can we ... ?'

'It will be difficult. We can write. Don't doubt me, darling Robert. If you hear reports about me, whatever they are, keep saying to yourself: *She does it all for me*. If you waver in this, you'll break my heart. It is steadfast and unchanging, but it is not indestructible. I have heard reports about you too, you know.'

And away Clara went to even greater successes. In Vienna

she was named the Royal and Imperial Chamber Virtuoso and showered with acclaim. Wieck, seeing her market value going through the roof, did all he could to corrode the prospect of marriage to Schumann. Clara, still just eighteen and susceptible to her father's will, began to echo his objections to Robert in her letters.

He realised he was fighting a battle on several fronts, and used his letters to keep his physical presence alive to her memory. 'I never leave you, but follow everywhere unseen,' he wrote. 'The figure fades away, but love and faith are unchanging.' On New Year's Eve, he reached to her in his solitude: 'Let us kneel together, Clara, so close that I can touch you in this solemn hour.'

Robert assessed his likely income and declared he was not far short of Wieck's stipulations. In response, he received a letter from the older man that tightened the noose: 'If I have to marry my daughter without delay to someone else, you will only have yourself to thank.'

~

Two further years went by.

Robert and Clara saw practically nothing of each other as they followed individual trajectories in the hope of swaying her father's escalating objections.

There were a few months of secret meetings that took place after Clara's return from Vienna, despite her father's vigilance. In the meantime, Wieck contacted Ernestine von Fricken in the hope of extracting some gossip about her old fiancé.

'Your old man is trying to get the dirt on me,' railed Robert.

Thank God, he thought, Wieck had not managed to track down Christel.

For a while the lovers relocated to the opposite corners of Europe: Robert to Vienna, where he hoped to become a publishing tycoon with the music review magazine he'd established years before and perhaps make a home for the eventual Schumann household; and Clara to Paris, without the company of her father this time, to try to become a lioness of its concert halls and salons. Again, the romance was maintained through correspondence: poems and affirmations, disputes and sweet making-up flying across the Continent in fast carriages.

Both hated where they found themselves. Clara was becoming exhausted by Friedrich's oscillations: in one letter he would declare she had been disinherited, in the next he wanted her to visit him. Robert deplored the Viennese; 'they are afraid of everything new!' he said. This was no place to pursue a business venture, especially when deep down he didn't want to be a businessman.

The endless machinations had become too absurd. Still apart, and with Clara's twentieth birthday approaching, the two decided to make one last appeal to Wieck.

Days later, Robert visited an attorney back in Leipzig.

'This has gone far enough with Herr Wieck!'

'And good morning to you, Mr Schumann,' said Herr Einert.

'We have spent years trying to winkle a consent out of him for his daughter and me to marry. Finally, he has said yes.'

'That is good news.'

'It is not. His conditions are as follows: we cannot live here while he is alive, that he keeps all of Clara's concert earnings for five more years, that he appoints someone to audit my financial affairs, and that Clara receives no inheritance. He wants us to sign an agreement to all this.'

'Well, it does sound a little draconian.'

'You are being too kind. So, I wrote to him again to try to bring our negotiations down to a realistic level. In reply, he sent his second wife around to my lodgings to tell me there would be no further discussion.'

'Which brings you to my door, I presume.'

'That is indeed why I am here. We have to take this bastard to court.'

~

Six months later, the local Court of Appeal met – again.

'This is the second meeting of the Court, and the third time we have considered this matter,' said the convenor. 'Herr Wieck, it is most helpful that you have deigned to appear before the Court on this occasion.'

Wieck stood up, looking unexpectedly nervous.

'I am here only because my daughter cannot see her way to agreeing with my latest and more accommodating conditions for approving her marriage to Herr Schumann,' he said.

'Given that you have barred her from your home, that may have been difficult,' said Einert.

'Of *course* I have! She is a fallen, wicked, abominable girl.' He spat the words in Clara's direction.

'May the Court hear these new conditions?'

'Certainly,' said Wieck. 'I request that she purchase all her belongings and piano from me, reimburse me the cost of my tuition from her childhood to now, pass on to her brothers her lifetime concert earnings, and have 8,000 thalers settled upon her by Herr Schumann in the likely event of their separation.'

'*Most* accommodating,' said Einert, drily. 'And why do you consider a separation is likely?'

'It is a question of Herr Schumann's character,' replied Wieck, his voice rising slightly. 'I would like to bring his deficiencies to the attention of the Court.'

'You are pressing charges? And these would be . . . ?'

'I accuse Schumann of being a bad composer. He has poor handwriting, his speech is often incomprehensible, he lies about his income and would have to be supported by my daughter. Finally, he is a drunkard.'

Schumann rose to his feet spluttering, his face flushing at what was clearly an inconvenient time.

'I'm sorry, Herr Schumann? We didn't quite catch that,' said the presiding judge.

'This is . . . *slander!*' Schumann's tone was surprisingly soft for somebody about to explode. Next to him, Clara's pale face tilted to one side, her eyes tinged with red. She was exhausted, and had fainted with stress before a concert appearance just days earlier when leaflets containing Wieck's description of Schumann were distributed to the audience.

'That is for the Court to decide,' said the judge. 'In the meantime, we will dismiss all of Herr Wieck's accusations – save that of drunkenness, which is a very serious charge. We will require proof, Herr Wieck.'

'Give me some time, and I will provide it,' Wieck said. His voice did not ring with confidence.

Schumann sat down shaking, again at an awkward moment. Sure, he liked a few glasses – but a *drunkard*? The music he was working on could not come from disordered thoughts, especially the *Arabeske*, which had so much of Clara's grace in it. And things were beginning to look up as far as his career was concerned; Franz Liszt just played part of the *Carnaval* in a recital. He began to think of who among his friends might testify to his sobriety. Mendelssohn came to mind.

Wieck glared at him as they passed while leaving the courtroom.

'I know how you live, Herr Schumann,' he hissed. 'And now the world will know. What there is of your career will be ruined – my daughter's also.'

Clara gripped Robert's arm, resolving to keep her tears to herself until she had returned to her mother, who had divorced Wieck years before.

'Do you think we shall be married in May?' she asked. 'It's only four months away.'

'Nothing can stop us now, my beautiful Clara,' said Robert.

~

Spring came and went, and still Wieck had not been able to provide the courts with the evidence to back his claims against Schumann. Incredibly, they gave him more and more time.

Meanwhile, Robert's head was brimming with ideas. Writing just for the keyboard was becoming too confining; he wanted to crush his piano. Nowadays, when he dreamed of the life that lay ahead, he felt a song coming on. Could a run at a symphony be far behind?

Finally, when the benign heat of a Saxon summer forced him to open his shirt collars while he worked, Schumann received the good news: Wieck had withdrawn his charges for want of hard evidence. It would be only a matter of time before the Court upheld their appeal. They had won – but they had also lost valuable time to be with each other.

At least it was not time wasted. Schumann knew that his musical powers had increased through hard work. He had progressed from a handful of works to his Opus 22, with two sonatas, the *Carnaval*, *Scenes from Childhood*, *Kreisleriana*, the *Novelletten* and the *Symphonic Etudes* among them. His imagination had been pushed in unexpected directions by the emotional tribulations Wieck had forced upon him. What had been better for his work – love, or the attempt to stamp it out?

He knew of creative artists for whom love was just a distraction, something that impeded their work. Those who had spent their lives without it were hardly *uncreative*: look at Beethoven. *Well*, thought Schumann, *I've swallowed the bitter pill of hopeless love for almost five years. In a few weeks I'm going to see what changes a consummated love will bring.*

When Robert and Clara married on 12 September 1840 at ten o'clock in the morning in a little church just outside Leipzig, the sun shone for the first time in many days. He remembered the lamplight that had illuminated their first kiss all those years before.

'This is the most beautiful day of my life,' she said.

Robert looked into her dark blue eyes and spoke as softly as always.

'Darling, we will play and bring joy to the world like angels.'

POSTSCRIPT

Robert and Clara were together for nearly fourteen years and had a family of eight children. He eventually made his name as a composer, while Clara struggled between pregnancies to maintain her reputation as one of Europe's greatest pianists.

In February of 1854 Robert talked of terrifying music playing constantly in his head, robbing him of sleep and threatening to drive him mad. On 27 February he left his house in a floral dressing gown and attempted suicide by throwing himself into the Rhine. At his own insistence he was taken to an asylum in Endenich. His young protégé Johannes Brahms moved into the Schumann household to help look after the children, where he promptly fell in love with Clara.

Schumann remained in care for the rest of his life. During that time Clara saw him only once, the day before he died on 29 July 1856, aged only forty-six. She outlived him by another forty years.

Present-day medical opinion suggests that the cause of Schumann's death was tertiary syphilis.

THE RETURN TO LIFE

Love, sex, delirium and a lust for revenge combined
into a Romantic nightmare for French composer
Hector Berlioz. A year after his futile infatuation for the
Irish actress Harriet Smithson became the subject of
the *Fantastic Symphony*, a betrayal by his new fiancée led
to actions stranger than anything he could put into his
music: a cross-dressing suicide mission across Europe
with a Parisian bloodbath as the intended finale.

~

*'I am getting on. No more rage, no more revenge, no more trembling,
gnashing of teeth, no more hell in fact!'*

Hector Berlioz (1803–1869) in a letter to his friend
Humbert Ferrand, 10–11 May 1831

APRIL 1831

Bells rang the Angelus across Florence as the composer tore open the letter in the poste restante office, unable to wait until returning to his hotel.

Already dishevelled from weeks of sleepless nights, he managed to become even more so within the duration of several paragraphs, tears starting from his eyes, his left hand stabbing a memorable shock of red hair.

'My dear Monsieur Berlioz ...' the letter began – not even from *her*, but from her mother, the person he thought soon to be his mother-in-law.

The salutation rang hollow at once. He was nobody's 'dear'; not when someone other than the person he loved wrote such a letter.

'... Camille is to be married immediately to Monsieur Pleyel, a union to which I have given my full consent. You must remember that I never formally agreed to your planned union with my daughter, so there can be no question of a breach of promise ...'

His hands trembled, almost tearing the letter apart.

'... Nevertheless, we appreciate this news will come as something of a shock to you. It is Camille's deepest wish that you may accept our decision in the nobility of spirit with which we believe you to be so richly endowed, rather than capitulating to more base emotions. Above all, we implore you not to consider anything by way of response that might endanger your personal safety or bring grief and humiliation to your family.'

Madame Moke was telling him not to kill himself.

Berlioz folded the letter. He was crying with rage and wanted to be sick, more from the realisation of a long-held suspicion than from genuine surprise. It was clear to him now just why Camille's mother had urged him to leave both Paris and his fiancée as quickly as possible after his victory in the Rome Prize; why her demeanour towards him had changed noticeably in the weeks before his coach started out on the long southern trip; why she insisted that the engagement needed to last as long as it might take for him to have his music make some serious money.

She had already found somebody with bigger pockets than his to be a son-in-law and wanted Berlioz out of the way before delivering this miserable coup de grâce.

What a duplicitous bitch, he thought. They could all go hang as far as he was concerned. He snorted, and a woman nearby whispered to her young daughter not to stare at the stranger.

Then the idea struck.

What to do next was so obvious, so clear, that he rushed into the street, his face a deathly white.

'Hector!' called a familiar voice. It was his architect friend Schlick. Berlioz slowed his pace and turned around.

'You've collected the mail ahead of me today ... my dear man, you look *appalling*!' Schlick said with sudden concern.

'Read this,' said Berlioz, handing him the letter.

Schlick studied its contents with mounting apprehension. He knew how much his mercurial friend adored the young woman whom he dubbed his 'Ariel'. To have a Shakespearean persona conferred on one was to occupy the highest position in Berlioz's pantheon; before this 'Ariel' there had been an unhappy attachment to an 'Ophelia' and he'd written music about both of them. The score of Ophelia's *Symphonie fantastique* (or *Fantastic*

Symphony) was still being revised back in his hotel room.

'Hector, this is monstrous,' said Schlick. 'Think clearly before you keep rushing about like this.'

'I've already left Rome and put my competition stipend at risk,' said Berlioz. 'It was sending me mad, the absence of any news from Paris since I came to Italy. The only way to get to the bottom of the mystery was to quit the Academy and head back. And now, voilà!' – he took the letter back from Schlick – 'It has been solved.'

'What happens now – back to Rome?'

'Right now I need some consolation, a place where I can try to get over this. My family live not far from Grenoble; if I leave immediately, I can be there within the week.'

'Of course, of course – you need cheering up. Some sleep, a few good meals, put all of this behind you. Let me help. You'll need a stamped passport and transport, and I know the authorities responsible. Get back to your hotel and pack; I'll sort the rest. There's a mail coach that leaves the Piazza della Signoria at six tonight. You're going to be on it.'

'Thank you, Benjamin. You've saved me. I don't think I could have answered for myself tomorrow.'

Schlick rushed away to make the arrangements. Berlioz watched his retreating figure, pleased that his lie had been believed and that no later accusation of complicity could be attached to his friend's assistance.

Hector was not returning to the bosom of his family.

Instead, he was going to Paris, where he would shoot three people before turning the gun on himself.

～

They would be expecting him back in Paris, surely. After hurling such a bomb, did they really think he wouldn't show up on their doorstep? The servants would already have been reminded of his startling appearance.

They would be expecting someone who looked like Hector Berlioz.

He crossed the Arno and found a French milliner's shop.

'Madame, I have a most unusual request, and a most pressing one. I need a complete lady's maid outfit made to my size, and I need it by five o'clock this evening. Can it be done? I will pay whatever is required.'

'*Your* size, monsieur?' She was only mildly surprised; a couple of her gentlemen clients had made similar requests. This was Florence.

'It is for a little comedy. Is this possible?'

'There will be a premium; I'm sure you understand. *Enrico!*'

The carefully groomed assistant ran the tape over Berlioz. 'Madame, we can make an adjustment to something in stock. Just a nip in at the hips,' he said appreciatively.

'A hat, too,' said Berlioz, aware that his hair would give the game away.

'In that case, a veil is essential,' said Enrico, realising that his client's sideburns would look even more conspicuous with a dress. 'Could I suggest that monsieur try something in green?'

'Done,' said Berlioz.

'And if monsieur should ever find himself in Firenze again with a little spare time . . .'

'I will be back at five.' The would-be drag artist swept out of the shop.

'An extra twenty francs should do it,' the milliner added. 'French men,' sighed Enrico.

~

Back at the Hôtel des Quatre Nations, Berlioz checked his armoury. He had brought two double-barrelled pistols with him from the Villa Medici in Rome, where his intention had been to go out shooting game on lazy weekends. In case of malfunction, he decided to have vials of laudanum and strychnine to hand for his own demise; to confess while dying was very – well, Shakespearean. Even a triple murder-suicide was entitled to a touch of poetry.

His symphony, the poor soon-to-be orphan, was not yet fully revised; there was still some sonic glitter to add to its ball scene. Berlioz scribbled some marginalia into the score to help a subsequent editor with its completion should it ever again be performed ('... *in the composer's absence*') and threw the sheaf of manuscript into a trunk with other effects to be despatched to his family after his departure.

Such was his clear sense of purpose that all of this had taken no time at all. Food? Unthinkable. Looking suspiciously homicidal, he prowled the streets of Florence, stopping to admire Cellini's *Perseus* in the Piazza della Signoria. The muscled warrior, sword in hand, held the decapitated head of Medusa aloft, the snakes of her hair still writhing.

She really had it coming, Berlioz thought to himself. *There is a majesty in vengeance. And that Benvenuto Cellini; he's my sort of artist. If I lived any longer I would have written an opera about him.*

At five p.m. he returned to the milliner's shop. The costume was ready, and when he tried it on, it fitted perfectly.

The milliner kept the change. 'Your comedy will be a great success, I'm sure, monsieur,' she said.

'If so, you are bound to read all about it,' Berlioz replied.

~

Schlick had kept his word. At six, Berlioz climbed aboard the coach with its cache of correspondence bound for Paris. Seeing the expression on his passenger's face, the driver decided that conversation would be pointless, even if they spoke the same language. All Berlioz noticed through the window in the darkening of evening was the worried expression of his friend. Behind Schlick, a final glimpse of Perseus' sword gave statuesque approval to his bloody plan.

It was quite simple, really. A lady's maid was sure to obtain entrance to the Moke ménage. Once inside, he would produce his primed pistols and despatch Camille's mother and fiancé with the same precision he employed on Italian quail. Camille's own end would have a little more theatricality; seizing her hair with one hand as if she were a Medusa, he would fling his hat and veil away with the other, declaim something to do with faithlessness, Hell and vengeance (Shakespeare could provide the right words), and then ensure her brains were removed from her head in as spectacular a way as possible.

Such a waste of a perfectly beautiful head, he knew. Almost exactly a year before, his friend Hiller had described Camille in an infatuated discourse.

'You should meet her, Hector,' he said. 'You'll understand

just why I am in love with her. It's platonic right now, but I'm working on it.'

'Why should I meet her?' Berlioz's mind was still full of the Irish actress with whom he'd been infatuated for more than two years, whose presence haunted the symphony he was now churning out at speed.

'I've told her all about you, and happened to mention the Harriet thing.'

'Ferdinand! Really!' Berlioz chided. His recent letters to Hiller had been written in giant scrawl over large pages, describing fresh bouts of torment.

'You *are* writing a symphony about the whole affair. Soon it'll be public knowledge. Anyway, Camille thinks your passion is inspiring. She says she'd *adore* somebody to love her with such intensity. I'm doing what I can in that department, but frankly, none of us is in your league, Hector. We wouldn't survive. Now and then I wonder if it's killing you. That last letter was hard to read.'

'It was harder to write.' Berlioz sighed. 'When do I see this muse of yours, then?'

'You already have, I presume. She teaches at the same finishing school you do. While you're plucking serenades on your guitar in one room, she's listening to piano scales in another.'

'*That* is your Camille? But she is *delightful*! Those eyes – and a true musician.'

'Just eighteen, with the world soon to be at her feet. She would be happy for you to introduce yourself as the notoriously famous lover.'

'Hiller, you are a coquette in a man's clothing. If you were a woman I would *hate* you,' said Berlioz, laughing.

Now and then Berlioz and Camille acknowledged each other as they passed in the corridors of Madame d'Aubré's school for young ladies. A glance, a nod of the head – that was all, both offered with an undeniable charm. *She is a spirit of the air*, thought Berlioz, already framing her as an Ariel.

One afternoon there was a knock at his studio door. He was surprised to hear Camille announce herself. She entered, her slim figure outshone by relentless blue eyes.

'This is unexpected, mademoiselle.'

'I don't see why, Monsieur Berlioz. Surely you have noticed the obvious by now. This conversation was always going to happen.'

He had noticed nothing for days except putting his Harriet theme in a country setting midway through the *Fantastic Symphony*. 'You will need to enlighten me. I have been distracted by my work of late.'

'From what I hear your distraction goes back several years, monsieur, and has been a fruitless one – apart from the music you are writing.'

'Well then, about what were we always going to speak?'

'The obvious.'

'Mademoiselle, you will need to place the obvious directly in my sight.'

'That is why I am here. This is what I am doing.'

'*You* are the obvious?'

'*Me*, monsieur. You have been so busy radiating passion that you fail to see passion when it comes your way.'

'Mademoiselle Moke . . .' Berlioz said, confused.

'*Camille* – please,' she corrected him. 'Camille, who is attracted to you. I think I am in love with you.' She took several steps towards him, her right eyebrow arched, slim pianist's fingers stroking her neck.

'This … this … cannot be. You have Hiller …'

'That is true – but *he* does not have *me*. And neither do you have Miss Smithson, as much as you might make her the star of your symphony, Monsieur Berlioz.'

He followed her glance to the scrawl of notes on his desk. Harriet's theme on woodwinds was plain to see, overlying the *tremolando* of violins and the bluster of cellos and double basses.

'You aren't *likely* to have her, are you?' she said, her voice hardening. 'Not while she is sleeping with her Romeos and her Hamlets.'

'That's absurd! You cannot know, cannot *speak* such a thing.'

'The backstage world is small, Monsieur Berlioz, even in a big city,' she said. 'Word travels fast.'

～

Berlioz's eyes narrowed while he relived that conversation in a mail coach rumbling through the Italian night. They stopped for an hour when he and his belongings were transferred to a fresh carriage and horses at a village staging post, and his papers presented to the sleepy clerk.

A tap on the shoulder broke his reverie.

'Pietrasanta, signore,' announced the coachman, hesitantly. 'After here it is dangerous; there are robbers. You have pistols, yes?'

Damn it! – he had noticed.

'That is good,' the driver continued. 'Please, signore – keep them uncapped and hide them under the seat cushions. You may need them on the next leg of the journey, but if they are seen too soon we could be murdered.'

Back on the road, memories prevented sleep. Hector remembered how he fled his room in total despair after Camille's accusations about Harriet's love life to roam the countryside north of Paris like a spectre, waking up the next morning in a ditch.

Everything was changed by Camille's sudden declaration, especially the course of his symphony. Its music now darkened from the pastoral setting to a scene of execution: his own, marching to the scaffold as punishment for Harriet's murder, a final recollection of her theme cut off by the fall of the guillotine blade. There would be no happy ending to this unrequited love for the now disgraced actress; she returned in the symphony's final movement as a witch, her distorted theme cackling on a high clarinet.

His feverish creation was an exorcism, rather than an act of revenge. Now that Harriet was gone, the completed symphony still hot on the page, there was room for something new. His studio door had opened; a bewitching sylph had stepped across the threshold – why not?

Later that day, he asked Camille to elaborate further on the 'obvious'. Within a few weeks, he had approached both her mother and his parents for their consent to marry. In June of 1831, unable to wait even another day for a positive response, the two music teachers eloped, making a short trip to Vincennes and the privacy of a hotel room.

'So this is what it is like,' said Berlioz, his heart slowing down after his orgasm.

Camille rolled onto her side, her eyes widening with surprise. 'Hector, are you telling me this is your first time? But you are twenty-six!'

Berlioz said nothing; he did not want to ask her the same question.

'Was Harriet anywhere in your thoughts just now?' There was confidence in her voice.

He smiled and stroked her unfastened black hair.

'Why would I waste my thoughts on the ordinary? She was never capable of understanding the loftiness of my feelings. I pity and despise her.'

~

'Genova, signore!'

Three days after leaving Florence, Berlioz had not spoken again to the driver; neither had he eaten anything, sustained only by his lust for revenge and a few sips of orange juice. The red stubble on his face accentuated his marble complexion, making him look like a sitting cadaver, bloodshot eyes blazing through the window of his carriage.

He was aware of a commotion outside, voices in some frenzied but hushed conversation. There was a timid rapping at his window, a gesture for him to step down onto the cobbled streets. The coachman looked puzzled and embarrassed.

'Signore, the luggage . . . it is not all here.'

What? Berlioz rushed to the rear of the carriage, counted the bags in the compartment that extended under his seat, and then reached into a side compartment similar to the one in Florence where he had stashed his lady's maid disguise for Paris.

The dress was missing.

He had been so lost in thought during the transfer in Pietrasanta more than forty-eight hours before that he had failed to notice some of the items had been left behind. By now, the wife or mistress of some village postal clerk would be proudly showing off her chic new outfit made in the Parisian style, complete with a charming green veil.

Fate be damned, Berlioz thought, wearily checking the contents of his wallet.

'Does anyone here speak French?' he called out.

Later, he and his translator exited the door of a local milliner, the fifth they had visited after being told repeatedly that his request was impossible. Inside, the *propriétaire* counted through the wad of French currency including a forty-franc tip and called together her seamstresses to have an emergency order for a lady's maid outfit ready for collection at five o'clock that same afternoon. As an added touch of style, the veil would be blue.

His legs like dead weights, Berlioz clambered slowly up a rampart overlooking the Mediterranean to try to refresh himself with sea air. As he stared down, the blue of the water felt as if it was enveloping him, washing away the turbulence of his thoughts, showing him the futility of his striving.

He recalled Macbeth's verdict on life:

'. . . A tale told by an idiot, full of sound and fury, signifying nothing.'

Yes, I am that idiot, he thought. *I am Macbeth, I am King Lear; it is all for nothing.*

His legs gave way – the endless blue was coming to meet him, taking him to the purity of nothing – he felt the cleansing rush of sea air, a slight impact, the blue entering him now, his sad tale soon over ...

Men were slapping his face, shouting at him in Italian and looking at each other with relief as they saw his chest heave.

He was lying in the bottom of a small fishing boat, his rescuers pointing to the spot on the high wall from where he had fallen – or had he jumped?

'You went under twice, signore,' one of them said. 'We made it to you with a fishhook just in time. Our catch of the day, *eh*?' They all laughed.

Bringing him to shore, they left him stretched out in the midday spring sun while he disgorged the blue water of the Mediterranean for an hour.

$\sim$

'Doesn't she *ever* intend to leave us alone?' Berlioz said to Camille, as they sat side by side on a settee in the Moke household the previous December. Her mother was pretending to make embroidery at a table nearby, her silence dominating the room.

'Hector, our little elopement all those months ago has tarnished your reputation for trustworthiness just a little,' Camille whispered. 'She wonders if your passion is that of a wholly *sane* man.' Before he could object, she called to her mother: 'Maman, you know of course that dear Hector loves me to distraction, don't you?'

'Monsieur Berlioz's distractions are famous around Paris,'

her mother said with what he felt to be a trace of acidity. 'Certainly, if anyone had told me that this is how lovers behave, I would not believe it to be true.'

'Merci, madame,' Berlioz said, unsure as to whether he had been complimented or not, but opting to give her the benefit of the doubt, since he was well on the way to meeting her preconditions for marriage. In the six months since that memorable night in Vincennes he had emerged as France's most promising young composer, winning the Rome Prize and unveiling his *Fantastic Symphony* with a spectacular concert just the week before. The new generation of artists, *his* crowd, loved the hallucinogenic cavalcade of wild emotions, the glittering ball, the sound of distant thunder in the countryside, the blood of a public execution, tolling church bells and the cackling of dancing witches – all describing the real-life love story everyone knew about. It was more than just a concert; it was a night at the theatre of the mind. Even his future mother-in-law was impressed, as was the teenager who accosted Berlioz as soon as the applause had died down.

'Franz Liszt,' he announced, idly brushing a mane of lank hair away from either shoulder. 'You've picked up where Beethoven left off. This calls for a drink.'

Camille too was eventually cast in a Berlioz work, floating through the stratosphere of glittering pianos, dancing to the chant of the chorus and soaring through the lightning brass and downpour of violins in his fantasia based on Shakespeare's *Tempest*, his Ariel in her true element.

'The poor French language cannot express how I feel, my darling,' he said one morning when she had connived to be away from home long enough for a bout of hasty lovemaking in his room. 'Give me an orchestra of a hundred and a chorus of a hundred and fifty and I will tell you.'

'That would be lovely, dear Hector,' she said, reaching down to guide his hand. 'But it would be ever so much more fun if you could touch me *here*.'

With Paris now presenting so many opportunities, his Rome Prize felt more like a banishment than a blessing. Berlioz could not understand why the authorities thought it necessary for him to decamp from France for the corked wine of Italian culture when the artistic life at home was providing him with champagne. 'I can learn more – *do* more – here,' he lamented to friends and fiancée. 'This will *stop* my career for two years, not start it.'

'Think of all the music you can write without worrying about money,' Camille said, not realising that all he would worry about was *her*.

'My daughter is right, Monsieur Berlioz,' said her mother in a tone of voice he detected as becoming cooler by the day. 'You've been given a great honour by the music establishment. Leave for Italy without delay, set the foundations for a profitable career, and everything else will take care of itself.'

Her advice was firm, but she could not meet his eyes; instead, she stared at her daughter, who in turn inspected the ring on her finger.

Berlioz was booked on a coach bound for Rome at month's end without knowing where his life was going.

~

'You're not going anywhere, Signor Berlioz,' the policeman said carefully while comparing this mad-haired apparition with the description in his papers. 'After your revolution in Paris last year, we don't trust the French not to bring trouble to the Kingdom of Sardinia. You are certainly not going via Torino.'

This was too much for the composer who had in the past few days endured the termination of an engagement, the loss of his luggage, and what any dispassionate observer would have called a suicide attempt, the last two of these mishaps incurred through an attempt to avenge the first. It was as if Macbeth's idiot whispered that Berlioz's sad tale was too delightful to end so soon.

'The gods will not persuade me to spare these baseless women,' Berlioz said to himself, the aftertaste of brine and vomit still in the back of his throat. 'I will destroy them – they must and they *shall* die.'

'*Scusi?*' said the policeman. 'My French, you understand ...'

'How do I leave this place to return to France?'

'I will give you a visa for Nizza, signore. You must take the coast road.'

'It's twice the distance, but let me have it, for God's sake. I'll go via Hell if I have to.' The long-defunct Catholic part of him suspected the infernal region was his final destination in any case.

His new outfit was ready as promised by the end of the afternoon and stashed into the side compartment of the Nice mail coach when it left Genoa at six. Berlioz, now wearing a change of dry clothes, rehearsed the Parisian denouement again and again, each time painting a little more blood and extruded brain matter onto the grim scene that would greet the gendarmes when they responded to the screams of the servants.

'Ah! A crime of passion,' one would say, inspecting the corpse with the pistol still clenched in its hand.

'*Mon Dieu*, it is the composer Berlioz, is it not?' would say the other, whose taste rose above the quotidian into the exalted world of high art and fashion.

'This is a tragedy of Shakespearean proportions,' the first might say – although as Berlioz conceded within seconds, it was far more likely he might not. 'The world has lost a great, creative spirit. Who knows what other masterworks he might have written?'

'And such style to die in that *fabulous* frock,' the second would conclude.

Berlioz became aware of something else in his mind as he stared into a stormy night and imagined the bloodshed to come: the sound of an orchestra, advancing upon him as if from a distance and becoming clearer by the second, cellos and basses playing a stentorian tune, falling away with exhaustion at the end of each phrase like the shouting of a very old man.

He searched his memory to find the source. Something from Beethoven, or a fragment from his beloved Gluck? Not that he could recall. It had come from nowhere; to be more precise, it had come from *him*.

Berlioz realised he was making something up. He was *composing*.

In the midst of this turmoil, embarking on a mission of murder, his mind flooded with rage, part of him was quietly assembling notes of music as if nothing was the matter.

He sat with his mouth open, eyes darting from side to side, striving to make sense of this pointless creativity. What was all this *telling* him?

There was a jolt when the coach came to a halt so that the driver could attach a drag to the wheels. Berlioz looked out into the turbulent darkness. They had stopped at the point where the Alps plunged into the sea and the road began a steep descent along the face of the cliff. He felt the immensity above him, the sea crashing at its base 600 feet below, the vehicle and its passenger perched on the ledge in between.

The impact of the waves carried up through the rock into the coach, through Berlioz's feet and legs, all the way to his core, each detonation blowing out another supporting pillar in the weakening construct of his rage, obliterating the image and stature of those he wanted to suffer. *Whoosh!* Madame Moke's opportunism turned to mediocrity. *Smack!* Camille's manipulative sexuality became the pathetic game of a sad little girl. *Bang!* Poor Pleyel didn't deserve a bullet; he would soon be in need of a funeral wreath and a consoling shot of brandy when he realised that all happiness in his life was gone.

There was a final explosion, not from the elements outside, but deep inside Berlioz himself, its plume rising faster and faster, bright colours coursing with a frantic energy. He had only a moment to understand it was the will to live before the ripples reached the top of his head and engulfed him with the most intense exaltation he had ever felt. The only way to expel the air and energy was to whoop into the night, yelling with joy and clutching the seat so as not to be blown out through the roof.

Outside, the driver heard the '*Ha!* Woo-HOO!' from inside

the coach, followed by laughter. *Uomo pazzo*, he thought. *I'll be happy to hand this one over when we get to Nizza.*

When the coach reached Diano Marina down near the shoreline, Berlioz dashed into a café with a new resolve and scrawled a letter to the Villa Medici back in Rome, explaining that he'd had an episode as the victim of an 'odious crime'. He promised to return, so long as his name had not yet been struck from the student register. He hadn't yet crossed the frontier into France, and would wait for a reply in Nice.

Berlioz felt an increasing lightness as each word landed on the paper, a dank fog being lifted with each stroke of the pen. The cellos and basses sang now through a hail of arpeggios falling from the rest of the orchestra, just like Berlioz had cried out in the preceding night's storm, celebrating a return to life.

Clarity came to all his senses. He listened to a sea more at peace on this morning, and saw a cloudless spring sky. He smelled the *boulangerie* next door and realised he'd eaten nothing since a long-ago breakfast in Florence.

My God, he was hungry.

~

'Where do you want to go, Frenchy-boy?' the girl said, putting down her last drink and giving him a conspiratorial smile.

Berlioz hadn't expected it to be this easy.

'My place has a great view of the sea, but there's the problem of the landlady,' he said. 'Why don't we go down to the beach?'

He had explored this part of Nice's coastline at length, stepping along pebbled beaches and taking refuge from the midday sun to steep himself in Shakespeare's *King Lear*. He saw now how close he'd come to being like the poor madman on the stormy heath, fixated on those who had been cruel to him, yet it had taken only an instant for Berlioz's world of thwarted love and all-encompassing hate to be dissipated by a shout from a cliff.

The letter from Rome contained good news. Years later he would remember these weeks in Nice as the happiest of his life.

How genuine had his love been, to vanish so quickly? How genuine his *hate*, for that matter? If they were monumental enough to have driven him to such extremes, why did their passage not last longer, feel more agonising? Was he guilty of the same fickleness as those whom he'd wanted to kill? Wasn't he more *sensitive* than they?

These were daytime questions. Right now was not the time to dwell on sensitivities; Berlioz was combing the beach under the moon looking to have sex with someone he'd known for four hours. After six months of abstinence he needed some relief, and the local girl had suggested she was more than happy to assist.

They stopped at the mouth of a cave Berlioz remembered from earlier that day.

'Let's go in here,' he called out over the wind and the crunch of the waves breaking on gravel.

'Fuck off,' grunted the couple inside.

There was nothing for it but to make a space on the beach itself. The night was warm, and the incoming tide would tickle at their legs.

Berlioz had never felt so alive. The cellos and basses he kept hearing *were* King Lear; now he had conceived Cordelia's beautiful oboe theme and the orchestral response to Lear's invitation 'Blow, winds, and crack your cheeks!' – even the pizzicato snap when the king's reason gives way.

Giggling, the girl exposed herself below the waist, scattering pebbles as she lifted her petticoats. Hector lowered his trousers and hoisted her bare right leg over his shoulder.

'Brace yourself, chérie,' he said. 'I feel an overture coming on.'

POSTSCRIPT

Berlioz returned to the Villa Medici for another year, staying until late 1832. Much as he disliked his time there, the Italian experience inspired several of his later works, including the *Harold in Italy* and *Romeo and Juliet* symphonies, the opera *Benvenuto Cellini* (about the casting of the Perseus statue), and the *Roman Carnival* overture.

The overture *King Lear* was completed at speed during his Nice sojourn and first performed in Paris in 1833.

Camille Pleyel was divorced by her husband in 1835, amid allegations of her repeated adulteries. The *Fantasia on Shakespeare's Tempest*, inspired by his idealisation of her as Ariel, eventually became the finale to his 'lyric monodrama' for narrator, soloists, chorus and orchestra called *Lelio, or The Return to Life* – the *Fantastic Symphony*'s official sequel.

DARK LOVE

Alessandro Stradella was brilliant, bad and dangerous to know during the Italian middle Baroque. Most fell under the spell of his music; women fell under the spell of the man. Hounded from a succession of cities by scandal, he made the mistake of coveting one particular woman and paid the price of stealing from a powerful man.

~

'Tis all too true that forever the stars rotate and with despotic tempers fling fierce disasters at me!'

Lucifer, in the *Christmas Cantata* by Alessandro Stradella (1639–1682)

VENICE, APRIL 1677

Stradella lifted the tip of his quill from the notes on his manuscript to admire his handiwork.

'Looks good, Alessandro,' he whispered to himself. 'Sounds even better.'

It was an aria for the Virgin Mary, singing of her love for the Christ Child:

Sovrano mio bene, mia spene, mio cor

He knew he had captured the stillness and expectation of the holy night with those violin suspensions in the first few bars. The drone in the lower strings and organ echoed the sound of the *pifferari* from the Abruzzo who piped their way into Rome at Christmas time.

Great pastoral effect, he thought. *Heaven knows what those shepherds played back in Jesus' time, but it won't have been as gorgeous as this.*

The kicker was the endless phrase of long notes trailing away to the stars, when Mary describes her maternal love, pouring like soft rain at the Child's feet:

L'interno suo amor con piogge serene riversa al tuo piè

... crowned by a stunning modulation that curled the whole thing away from the tonic.

Virgins always brought out the best in him.

'*Magic*, old son,' Stradella said again. 'Shit, I'm good. This is going to be one *hell* of a Christmas cantata.'

He had thought as much about himself earlier that morning. Sloshing the warm water around his face after shaving, he stopped to appraise his chiselled features, full lips and caramel eyes, concluding that he wasn't doing badly for a man in his thirty-eighth year. Women often gave him a second look as he passed them in the thoroughfare along the Grand Canal. All it took was a raised eyebrow and a slight tilt of his regal head, and the lady in question would check they were unobserved before following the straight, lean figure into an alley, away from the hubbub. The silent coupling took place beneath a canopy of hanging laundry, surrounded by dank smells and the mewing of cats.

It was all so easy in Venice, he mused. The sex felt so *urgent*. Maybe everyone thought they would sink into the lagoon if they wasted any time.

Stradella had only been in Venice for a couple of months, after fleeing from Rome when word got out about the money he and the castrato Vulpio had extorted from an old prostitute, the price for getting her hitched to Cardinal Cibo's nephew. They'd spent a good part of the 10,000 *scudi* she'd forked out getting the silly bastard pissed enough to go through with it.

Christ, but she was ugly, he remembered with a smirk. Probably no surprise that the cardinal was splenetic with rage. A bad look for the family, he said. He *was* the Pope's secretary of state, after all.

There'd been a knock on Stradella's door late one night.

'*Signore!*' Guido had urged him awake. 'There are men coming after you! They come from the cardinal!'

He knew precisely what was in store if he didn't get moving there and then. It was an inelegant way to skip town – grabbing what he could, having Guido throw a hastily packed chest into a wagon, leaving some tasty commissions up in the air – but it would have been even more inelegant to be found dead in the morning.

'Well, *that* was a fucking waste, Guido,' he complained as

they jostled out of the city in the back of the wagon, baggage strewn around them. 'Ten years of my life in this town – all gone. Writing for the Queen of Sweden. Being made an honorary servant of the Pope. Working my arse off for rich people who never pay. Then, when I finally score a bit of cash from someone who won't even notice it's missing, the Church sets out to kill me. I ask you – where's the charity?'

He thought of the boneheads ransacking his apartment even as he spoke, probably finding some letters from women that might give them a thrill – presuming they could read.

Thank God for patrons like Polo Michiel up in Venice. 'Alessandro, if you ever decide to relocate ...' he'd written any number of times. 'They'll love you up here. You'd have more work than you could handle.'

Stradella floated into town that February, the place misty and grey, the constant peals of church bells amplified by their reflections from the water. Stepping ashore onto what the Venetians considered dry land, he found himself inside a world of anonymity. The Carnival was in full swing, people wearing pale masks as they coursed around San Marco and the Rialto – priests, gamblers, the high-living sons and daughters of the aristocracy; everyone except the shopkeepers and those too poor to indulge in the licensed fun. Nine months from now, the front doors of the foundling homes would take delivery of a new generation of newborns, some of whose fathers would be in churches nearby, saying Mass and taking confessions.

Stradella imagined he too must be the father of a fair few bastards after some of his wild nights in Rome, and that he was probably going to have added to the tally of swollen bellies in

La Serenissima once the mists rose and the masks came off. Polo Michiel was right: in Venice, they *did* love him. The end of Carnival saw no respite from pleasure either. Alessandro was even more attractive without a disguise.

~

He held out the letter to Polo Michiel.

'His *niece*?' he said. 'I should be composing, not giving instructions to bored relatives.'

Stradella's friend winked, noting the florid calligraphy, doubtless the work of a scribe, and the wax seal in place of a signature at the bottom of the document. The bearer of the ring that made that imprint was someone whose request could not be ignored.

'It's from the Doge, no mistake,' Michiel said. 'Alvise Contarini. We say "niece" to explain the fifty-year difference in their ages. She's his mistress; at least, that's his intention. When you're approaching the end of your eighth decade, it must be a consolation to know that someone like her is waiting in your room.'

'Why does he want her to learn music?'

'Who knows? Perhaps he wants her to sing him to sleep.' Michiel winked again. 'Maybe she's expressed her own interest in the subject. It's more likely she fancies the new musician in town.'

'How clever of her to arrange for her protector to pay for a younger man's company – if she is indeed that strategic.'

'You don't become a doge's mistress by just batting your eyes. Then again, this *is* Venice.'

'Babysitting a rich man's spoilt brat takes me away from more important work.' Stradella sighed. 'I suppose I have no choice. My hourly rate won't be cheap, though.'

'You could charge interest,' said Michiel. '*Not* the sort of interest for which you're famous, Alessandro. You don't want to deal with a cuckolded doge.'

Three days later, a large gondola drew up outside Stradella's apartment. A small figure draped in a veil was escorted to his door to be admitted by Guido.

'Signore? Your guest has arrived.'

'Show her in,' said Stradella, uninterested. He was doodling with the vocal line in a solo motet. Putting down the quill, he turned to greet the visitor.

She entered, the line of her slim body delineated by a simple emerald green bodice. When she removed her veil, the hair clustered in loose curls around her ears was a rich auburn. It was the fashion for those who could afford it, but Stradella could see from the colour at the root and the paleness of the skin along the middle parting that Agnese Van Uffele presented just as Nature had made her.

If she was the sort of young woman to have contrived this situation, it wasn't apparent in her face: a high smooth forehead, an expression completely devoid of insolence, and a mouth that already threatened to break into a smile, revealing unusually good teeth for someone in their early twenties. Her eyes were the hazel of her hair type, with flecks of green made more apparent by the colour of her dress.

Stradella decided that he would enjoy teaching music to his new pupil.

For her part, Agnese quickly understood why the rumours about his sudden arrival in Venice might be true. He was almost improbably handsome, with a body whose obvious strength and leanness was quite different to the sagging corpulence she saw around the court, or the limpness of her lover's genitals she occasionally had to fondle, a spectacle made even more melancholy by flickering candlelight. She noticed Stradella's violin on a side table, the hairs of its bow alongside stretched taut, ready to make music. Just like its owner, she presumed.

There was already some sort of tension in the room, even though Stradella himself seemed unaffected by it. Agnese sensed it coming from his eyes as they ranged up and down her body. There was nothing in her appearance that was indecorous on this morning – the Doge's valet had made sure of it – yet she felt that even twice as many layers of clothing would feel just as transparent.

His gaze finally rested on hers. *Eyebrows*, she thought. *Can a man's eyebrows really be that intoxicating?* And their tapered shape! She would love to stroke them, just once. *What on earth am I doing here?*

'You are most welcome, signorina. I'm pleased to know the Doge will now have music to hand when needed.' The voice was as dark as the thick hair only just streaked with grey, despite the financial worries of his Rome years.

'It is an honour for me, Signor Stradella. The art of music has always brought me much pleasure. The Doge believes my receiving instruction from an esteemed musician of your experience may help me to extend that same pleasure to others, His Excellency in particular.'

Stradella crossed his arms, resting his right arm on his chest with fingers spread in such a way that she could easily guess at its contours. It would be a fine chest, she concluded.

'You must tell the Doge for me that it is *I* who am honoured to be chosen as the one to increase his pleasure, although I can't believe that having you in his company wouldn't be pleasure enough for His Excellency.'

She blushed, and the colour made its way down her long neck. Stradella was no fool; he could guess at the nature of her relationship with Contarini. She realised that the blush was less from embarrassment and instead a reaction to the way his lips caressed the word 'pleasure'.

Agnese knew she must decide quickly if the situation was already too dangerous. She could leave now, return to the Doge and tell him that Stradella had reluctantly concluded her talent was insufficient to the task of performing music at the level of His Excellency's expectation. The Doge might even be relieved she wouldn't be seeing the glamorous stranger.

She was jolted back to the moment by Stradella's voice. He had approached her.

'I take it you wish to read music, to sing?'

The situation was *extremely* dangerous. *It's very nice, this danger.*

'I'm told my voice is pleasant.'

'May I?' He reached for her face. She jerked back, a reflex.

'This is important, madame,' he said. 'If we're to make you a singer, I must have some idea of the quality of the instrument.'

Recomposing herself, she leaned forward to him, chin uplifted. He raised his hand again and touched her top lip with his middle finger, tracing its outline with a butterfly's lightness. When he reached the corner of her mouth she parted her lips slightly. Stradella saw the moist tip of her tongue and savoured the sweetness of her breath, so different from that of the merchant's wife he had screwed the day before.

His finger continued its journey along Agnese's lower lip, and she closed her eyes to concentrate on the sensation. The light pressure continued south, sliding over her chin onto her neck, thumb and forefinger either side of her windpipe. Another sensation was making itself felt, a tingling between her legs.

She reared again, this time from a man's voice outside hailing a friend across the narrow canal.

Her eyes opened. She and Stradella laughed. He withdrew his hand, brought the middle finger to his mouth, and very deliberately kissed the tip.

'It is a delicate instrument, madame. A refined orifice. We should give it a try, I think. Twice a week, beginning as soon as possible?'

It's now or never, Agnese. Say no. Take up embroidery.

JUNE

'It's called a *concerto grosso*,' Stradella said, attempting to unroll the manuscript pages along Agnese's naked back. 'A *big* concerto. We have so much opera in Venice, so much opera *everywhere*. I want to create something exclusively for instruments that has the same theatricality, a dialogue between ensembles of different sizes. Why should singers have all the fun?'

'That's a rather strange question to ask at this point in our studies,' said Agnese, reaching over to caress his arm. 'You've spent six weeks teaching me a lot about fun, and not very much about singing.'

'It came as some surprise to me to see that you knew so little about either. What on earth do you *do* in the Palazzo Ducale with that doge of yours?'

'Less than you think. The Doge is still vigorous in mind, but the rest of him is not really up for fun, and I mean that in every sense. You're the first man I've ever seen in such a – state. *This* state, I mean,' she said, running her hand along the topic of conversation.

'How does a beautiful local virgin end up as a decoration in a doge's palace? Or is that a silly question?'

'Not at all. It isn't the usual destination for local virgins, even though it's quite common for doges.' She frowned. 'My father is what you'd call a failed nobleman who poured what little remained of the family fortunes onto the gaming tables along the Grand Canal. When the cards took it all, he played his last hand by presenting me at court. He let it be known to the Doge's attendants that anything might be possible in exchange for the settlement of his debts.'

Stradella clasped her neck with concern. 'He *sold* you?'

'*Loaned* me, perhaps. Given the Doge's frailty, my father felt the essential part of the transaction – my virginity – wasn't likely to be violated. The contract would be terminated by the Doge's death sooner rather than later.'

'That's probably not how the world sees it, or you. I hope the family finances are restored.'

'They are – for now. We can enjoy a genteel poverty until the tables reopen with the next Carnival. This may all happen again. Fortunately, I have two younger sisters.'

'So, there you are, rattling around in his apartments, being a virgin – until recently.'

'The views of the lagoon are beautiful. And it's not entirely innocent. He likes me to show myself to him. Sometimes he asks for the warmth of my mouth. The sensation obviously gives him pleasure; I can hear it, but I certainly don't see it.'

Stradella looked away. Really, family 'honour' was such a putrid thing if it had to be preserved in ways such as this. How many times had he seen something similar in the great villas of Rome? This wouldn't end well for her, he knew. She had to be saved.

Hazel eyes flecked with green drew him back.

'You give him comfort without satisfaction,' he said. 'Unpleasant for you, frustrating for him.'

'For him to feel merely comforted seems to be enough,' she said. 'That doesn't mean he intends to be understanding about how *I* might be satisfied. The Contarinis are a large clan, possessive and jealous. They wouldn't hesitate to kill you if they knew about this. You're stealing one of the family jewels.'

'I can't count the number of times it's been stolen these past few weeks. I must say, being robbed suits you.' He laughed, releasing the scroll of music so that it snapped back into a loose cylinder, and trailed his fingers along the cleft of her buttocks, bringing them to rest on the dampness between her thighs.

'I'm so glad you've got that concerto out of the way, as beautiful as it undoubtedly will be,' she said, rolling onto her side and resuming her grip on him. 'Here's another *grosso* that awaits performance. Where's your violin bow?'

'Just the bow?' he said, handing it to her. 'What, no violin?'

'*I'll* be your violin,' she said, propping up her leg and touching the bow's horsehair lightly against her vulva. 'You stroke me, and I'll sing.'

He snatched it back. 'That is *horsehair*, my little fiddler. Fine for a gut string, but not for an instrument as delicate as yours.' Moistening his index finger, he continued, 'Your song will be sweeter if we turn you into a glass harp.'

THE DOGE'S APARTMENT

Alvise Contarini was waiting for Agnese when she returned.

The day's last light filled the room from the reflection of the lagoon and bounced off the Doge's bald head, freed at last from its hot prison of the ducal hat. His expression had the smug petulance of an old man who knows what he knows.

'At *last*, signorina,' he said. 'Young Agnese has had a busy day.'

She blushed. This sounded too much like an accusation.

'Indeed, my lord. One loses all sense of time passing when one is singing.'

'Singing – *again*? With your music teacher, the composer – Signor Straddle.'

'Stra*della*, my lord.'

'Of course, of course. Close, but not quite. What was I thinking? You've been singing a great deal of late, my dear. Whenever I ask for you, my equerries tell me that you're away – *singing*.'

'Signor Stradella tells me that I have a great talent for it, my lord.'

'And yet I've not heard you sing a note, despite the considerable sum I have paid for your education.'

His eyes, rheumy with age and fatigue, suddenly drilled into hers.

'I think we should *all* have the privilege of celebrating your new, great talent – don't you think?'

'I d-don't know, my lord . . .'

'You are obviously bringing great delight to your teacher, reputed to be one of the greatest in Europe. I've been enquiring about Signor Saddle's history these past days – and I've heard so many *interesting* things about him. His credentials for the instruction of young women are renowned.'

Agnese turned a deep crimson.

'We will gather a few people in the Scarlet Chamber – let's say, tomorrow evening. Since you now read music so well, I will arrange for a notated song to be placed before you on a stand. We will allow you two minutes to peruse it, and then – you will *sing* it! Something pleasant and local, but not anything you can know. What do you think? I'm sure we'll all be *amazed*.'

'My lord, I'm too shy to perform for such a large group.'

'*Nonsense*, my dear Agnese. Bring your teacher as well. I *insist* upon it. He must be *so* proud of you by now. He should be accountable for whatever it is we are to hear, don't you think?'

'My, my v-voice is just a little tired from all this work . . .'

'You're a strong young woman and you will bounce back,' he said. 'I can't *imagine* what we'd all think if you were to refuse to honour us in this way. It would make all the lessons you've received from Signor Stradalliance seem like *such* a waste of time. I should want to have words with him! But right now, you need something warm for that throat of yours.'

Struggling onto his ancient feet, Contarini laboriously took down his breeches.

'Something like *this*,' he said, pointing.

~

'We have only today,' Agnese gasped, her voice choking with panic. That morning's gondola had travelled at speed from its mooring near San Marco.

'Fuck me dead,' said Alessandro.

'I think that about sums it up.'

'What are our options? Apart from being killed, I mean.'

'I suppose I could *try* to sing this evening,' she said.

'You're a brave girl,' he said, 'and you are perfectly wonderful at certain things, as we've discovered these past six weeks. Singing, however, is not one of them. My dear Agnese, I've not said this before because your doge's money has been handy, and because I didn't want to discourage your good intentions. The fact is, you are clearly tone deaf. If you utter more than two notes in front of that crowd, we'll never leave those apartments alive.'

'Oh,' she said, dismayed for only a moment before recollecting what their lessons had really been about. 'In that case, we must leave here – *now*.'

Stradella rolled his eyes. This was most inconvenient.

'Agnese, I've been here in Venice only four months! There is the very real prospect of my being commissioned to write an opera for next year's Carnival. Would you have me throw that away?'

Her panic was returning. 'Alessandro, if we stay, you'll still have *lived* in Venice for only four months.' She took one of his hands and pressed it to her forehead. 'I *beg* you, signore. Take me away from that man and this place.'

He looked at her with a surge of affection and something else that surprised him: a sense of responsibility.

He recalled what he'd thought the day before.

She has to be saved.

His own course of action was just as clear. *Leave, or suffer the consequences.*

They had a matter of a few hours; perhaps less, if the Doge was curious even now about where Agnese had gone.

But go where?

His mind trawled through the gallery of aristocrats with whom he'd been close in Rome, and by extension their network of friends, those to whom he knew he'd been recommended. There were pockets of them studded in other states, nobles who seemed interested in his work.

One name stood out. She was intelligent, musical, and newly installed as regent. Word had it that she might even be persuaded to be more interested in the man than his music.

Maria Giovanna, born Marie Jeanne Baptiste of Nemours – head of the Duchy of Savoy.

It was a stretch – almost as distant as Rome – but they would head westward, far from the Papal States where his name was still mud, closer to France. Maria would offer them protection; he could tell. In time, Polo Michiel might even give him some help, maybe introduce him to a few of the really cashed-up crowd. The whole escapade could be a professional goldmine.

'Agnese,' he said, cradling her head, 'we are going. *Guido*!'

The call brought his servant to the door within seconds.

'Guido, pack as much as you can in the next hour and call me a gondola. We're quitting town.'

Guido looked at him with disbelief.

'But – *where*, Signor Stradella?'

'Savoy. And make sure my violin bows are packed safely. Agnese is coming with us.'

SEPTEMBER

Contarini squinted at the scrawl on the letter before handing it back to Polo Michiel.

'What is this, you say?' he barked.

'A request, my lord,' Michiel replied. 'From Stradella. He asks me for letters of recommendation. I thought you should know.'

The Doge smiled broadly, exposing most of his gums and their single remaining tooth.

'You did well, Polo Michiel,' he said. 'There's been talk about your friendship with the musician. It wouldn't have been good for your *reputation* in Venice if I'd learned this information had been withheld from me. You understand what I am saying?'

Michiel understood only too well. The Doge's anger over his cuckolding and public humiliation by Stradella was the talk of the Grand Canal. Contarini wanted blood. Those known to be in the composer's Venetian circle were beginning to think theirs would be the first spilled. Polo couldn't believe his luck when Stradella's letter arrived. He would reply, of course. Meanwhile, it was a lifeline; a ticket to redemption.

Contarini's cold voice cut through his sense of relief.

'*She* is with him?'

Stradella had said as much in a note accompanying the letter.

'Yes, my lord. I believe that not even her father knows.'

'You are correct, Michiel. I have been questioning him. *Vigorously.*'

No wonder I haven't seen the poor bastard for a while, thought Michiel.

'And from *whore* does this letter come to you, my trusted friend?'

Michiel recoiled at the last three words. Their insincerity felt obscene. He was sickened at having to answer this one inevitable question, aware of what might happen to his friend. But there were many canals in Venice, and a corpse could lie beneath their cold waters for some time before rising to the surface – even at this time of year.

'Turin, my lord.'

Contarini studied his fingernails. Clean as a freshly drawn blade, he noted.

'Turin, eh? Well, he's a cheeky one, that Saddle fellow. You know what, Michiel? I've *always* wanted to go to Turin, especially in summertime. I might take a few friends – do a little business.'

TURIN

It was quiet and dark when Stradella heard his name called from the street. When the composer roused himself and took the envelope from the messenger, he saw it bore the seal of the Archbishop of Turin. Its contents soon woke him up.

'Maestro Stradella,' it began, 'a team of men from Venice led by His Excellency the Doge, Alvise Contarini, are but nine miles distant from Turin and will arrive in the morning. You should be in no doubt as to their purpose. It is my belief that you are in mortal and imminent danger. Therefore, I have made arrangements for you to seek sanctuary this very night. You, signore, are expected at the church of S. Domenico, while the Signorina Van Uffele is awaited at the convent of S. Maria Maddalena.'

'Fucking marvellous,' said Stradella. '*Guido!*'

Agnese's face was pale in the lamplight from lack of sleep as she prepared to hurry away through the backstreets.

'Alessandro, I'm almost as scared of being *inside* the convent as feeling unprotected on the outside. There are many girls who never reappear through those doors. Sometimes a love of God has nothing to do with it.'

'You must go, Agnese,' he said, trying to sound as concerned as possible. They had been in each other's company the entire time in Turin, and there was nothing more he could teach her. He was bored.

~

Late the next morning, the Archbishop of Turin glared across his desk at the visitor.

'I am of course honoured to receive you, Your Excellency,' he said. 'However, it is a most *unusual* matter that warrants the attention – indeed, the *visitation* – of a Venetian doge. And you have not announced yourself to our regent?'

Maria Giovanna would not be happy when he told her, he knew. This was tantamount to a foreign invasion.

'I did not think the purpose of my visit was appropriate enough to arouse the interest of your court,' said Contarini with false delicacy. 'You have received the documents?'

The archbishop nodded. The early delivery of Contarini's stipulations had enabled Stradella to be tipped off and squirrelled to safety.

Contarini continued. 'My conditions are clear, I trust.'

'They are, although one *could* argue that your issuing them during the course of a precipitate appearance in a neighbouring city-state makes them look ... well, *unreasonable*.'

'My dear archbishop! All I wish to do is relieve Savoy of a fugitive from Venetian justice. You are doubtless aware there are reputational issues at stake.'

'Your Excellency, the *fugitive* in question is here at the pleasure of Her Highness. I don't think she will be happy about an unexpected delegation of Venetians demanding the deportation of one of her favourite guests, especially when the person in question is providing music for the court. You have no proof of this man's alleged crimes.'

Contarini's voice hardened. 'The *proof*, Your Grace, is a certain young woman who is in his company.'

The archbishop could barely conceal his smile. He affected a more jocular tone.

'Signor Stradella is an extremely handsome man, Your Excellency. I would be surprised if he were to spend his time alone. This young lady is from Venice?'

'Indeed.'

'And a relative of yours?'

Contarini knew he was being patronised. 'We both know that is not the case.'

'Of course. Her father is also here now. He limped in from Venice several weeks ago. Rather the worse for wear, I might add, after talking with your equerries about his daughter's whereabouts. You Venetians take your reputation very seriously, it seems.'

The Doge's mouth tightened, then relaxed into its largely toothless smile.

'I am concerned about the reputation of *your* jurisdiction, Your Grace. It would be unfortunate if Turin were to be branded as a place that condones immorality.'

Coming from the Doge of Venice, the archbishop thought this a bit rich. On the other hand, he witnessed such hypocrisy every day. There was no need to protest. He could see the Doge was leading to something.

'Where is the young lady now?' Contarini said.

The archbishop saw no reason to lie. Any foreign contravention of his wishes would be an act of war.

'She is installed in one of our convents, Your Excellency.'

The Doge narrowed his eyes and tilted his head back. *Because you put her there for safety ahead of this conversation, sly old priest.*

Spreading his hands in a conciliatory gesture, much like a man of the cloth, he pretended to have a sudden inspiration.

'Very well, let us salvage *all* our reputations – including that of the young lady, whose location suggests the solution.'

'Your Excellency . . . ?'

'I propose that Her Highness should be sufficiently displeased with one of her guests living openly in sin to withdraw all of her commissions from him.'

'*Sack* him?'

'Not quite. Merely postpone any further work until he rectifies his immoral situation.'

'I see. And Signorina Van Uffele's options are . . . ?'

'She renounces her claim to being a Venetian citizen and stays in your convent by taking the veil.'

'It is a noble solution, Your Excellency – but she may not wish to do so.'

Contarini snarled with relish as he saw his coup de grâce.

'Then Signor Stradella must make an honest woman of her.' He knew what the roving musician would think of that: a form of death. *But not quite. I still have other plans.*

'As a man of God, I have no problem with this, Your Excellency.'

'You are a wise man, Your Grace.'

He motioned the archbishop to stand, and the two walked over to the window of the study overlooking the large cobbled courtyard.

Below them, forty men – mainly Contarini family members and a few hired thugs – were dismounting from their horses and checking their weapons: swords and daggers.

Contarini turned to his host. 'If this choice can be exercised upon my fugitive, I will leave Turin immediately without any further demands,' he said. 'That is, as soon as my men have enjoyed some of your city's hospitality.'

TURIN, 10 OCTOBER

Stradella lifted the tip of his quill from the marriage contract and grimaced at his signature.

'Congratulations, signore,' said the notary in the study at Santa Maria Maddalena.

The composer shrugged. 'Commiserations, more likely,' he said. 'A man has to work. My career in this city would be over otherwise.'

The mother superior beamed. 'We are sorry to say goodbye to our novitiate, but she will be happy about this. It is late. She can stay with us tonight and be with you in the morning.'

Stradella thanked her and left, taking a route on foot along a colonnade outside the convent. The nights were drawing in, but there would be warmth inside the tavern where he was due to meet Lucia. He would have to explain his changed circumstances to her. Would she mind? *If so – too bad.*

Two men stood against a column at the far end and watched the approaching figure.

'That's him,' said one.

'He's pretty well built,' said the other. 'Might put up a fight.'

'Funny,' said the first. 'You always expect those artistic types to look a bit frail.'

'Artistic?'

'Sure. He's a composer. He writes music. My wife heard

some of it in church back in Venice.'

'What was it?'

'I think she said it was a cantata or something. She swore she could hear the angels weeping, it was so beautiful.'

'Big fucking deal. What's a cantata?'

'Buggered if I know. But you know why we're doing this.'

'He ran off with the Doge's girl, didn't he?'

'Sure did. Only after he'd fucked half of the women in Venice.'

'I hope your wife was safe, then. Now, *that's* impressive.'

'You bastard.' He laughed. 'Let's get on with it. Remember: when it's done, we're supposed to go to the French ambassador's and claim asylum.'

'Got it. We're using knives?'

'*No* knives. The Contarinis want it to be slow.'

Stradella glanced at the two men while passing, just in time to see one of them raise a fist. He jumped back, parried the blow and reached for his own dagger.

The reflex wasn't fast enough to stave off the second man's kick to his groin. The composer felt the pain suck the air from his lungs. His legs began to crumple. Finally extracting the knife from its scabbard, Stradella swivelled enough to slash wildly through the air, the arc of the blade catching one of the men across the cheek. The wound was superficial, but had a sting.

'You *fucker*,' the man said angrily. The two closed in on Stradella as he slumped onto the flagstones, raining kicks and punches upon their quarry until their fists were slimy with his blood.

Postscript

The near-fatal beating of Stradella became an international diplomatic incident when Maria Giovanna of Savoy complained to the French King Louis XIV about his ambassador's complicity in the illegal actions of a foreign power.

After his recovery, Stradella left Turin, arriving alone in Genoa in early 1678. Nothing more was ever heard about Agnese Van Uffele.

His reception in the port town was more welcoming. A group of nobles provided an annuity for the provision of a house and fellow servant to Guido. Commissions came in by the boatload, including one from a Roman duke for an opera set to Stradella's own libretto, called *Dark Love*.

Stradella was stabbed to death on 25 February 1682 in Genoa's Piazza Banchi. He was forty-two. The assassin's identity and reasons for the murder remain unknown. It was rumoured at the time that the composer was having an improper relationship with a married woman of the influential Lomellini family.

LOVED TO DEATH

Richard Wagner was the most controversial composer
who ever lived His masterpiece, *Tristan and Isolde*,
foreshadows psychoanalysis in peeling back the layers
between the external world and the unconscious.
For Wagner, there was only one way to prepare for
his exploration of transcendent love ...

~

*'Since I have never in my life enjoyed the real happiness of love,
I wish to create a monument to this, the most beautiful of all dreams,
in which this love shall have its proper fill, from beginning to end.'*

Richard Wagner (1813–1883) to Franz Liszt, 1854

ZURICH, APRIL 1857

'I'm going to call this place "Asyl" – short for asylum – because
it will be a refuge,' said Richard Wagner, doffing his velvet
beret. He looked for the first time through the freshly painted

windows of the house and across the patch of garden to the waters of the lake beyond, dulled by the rain of early spring.

There was a clatter of activity in the entrance hall as their luggage was brought in from the carriage outside.

'This is all unbelievable, Richard,' said his wife, following him into the room, patting her chest to calm her palpitations. 'These people must adore you.'

'The Wesendoncks know how much the world will benefit from their common sense in giving me the space I need for my work,' he announced.

'By common sense, I presume you mean generosity?' said Minna, knowing that gratitude was something Richard considered the sentimental reaction of lesser mortals.

'That too,' said Wagner. 'Their demands are modest. Herr Wesendonck is asking for a peppercorn rent of only a thousand francs a year.'

'It probably *is* modest by the standards of accommodation around here,' said Minna, aware that the cottage was a small place in a rich neighbourhood, 'but still more than we can manage. How will you pay?'

'I won't, of course. After all, the world owes me a living, and the Wesendoncks are the ones honoured to repay this debt at present. One day they will boast that Wagner was their tenant.'

Bloody Richard, she thought. *If we're not careful, he's going to put us back in the same position we've suffered time and time again: letters from the creditors, a summons from the bailiff, the inevitable midnight flit out of town with our belongings and the dog crammed into a cart.*

And that was often the *best* outcome; sometimes the Wagners weren't even that lucky. In Paris, Richard had ended up in a debtor's prison while his wife passed the hat around.

Minna sighed, thinking yet again she should really have stayed with the businessman who lured her away just six months after she and Wagner were married. Life would have been so much easier. Instead, they had been virtually homeless after only just getting out of Dresden in the wake of the uprising there in 1849, Richard with an arrest warrant over his head, a political exile who dreamed of changing the world by writing an enormous series of works about its destruction, all the time spending every penny he could cajole from starstruck admirers, many of them women. Oh yes, Minna knew something about *them*.

One of those admirers was Otto Wesendonck, a wealthy silk merchant who had encountered Richard at the Hotel Baur au Lac up the road some years earlier. The successful capitalist held anti-monarchist views similar to those of the artistic revolutionary, and soon Richard was casting his spell, describing his vision for the future of music and drama and its liberating impact on the world. All it would take for this vision to become a reality were a few loans while he waited for his circumstances to improve, or until the cheques rolled in from the theatres of Europe. It was inevitable, Wagner believed.

Otto obliged in the form of a large advance against future performance royalties. Now came this – an offer of the small house adjacent to the sprawling Wesendonck estate, where the building of a new grandiose villa for its owners was almost finished. Richard would become the captive creative spirit at the bottom of a rich man's garden.

Nobody was happier at the prospect of such a ménage than Otto's young wife, Mathilde. Minna could see that Mathilde was infatuated with Richard. It was obvious in the way she stared at him when he launched into one of his tiresome set pieces about reforming the theatre by returning to ancient Greek models, or the need to shatter present-day operatic conventions, or how dogs were better companions than people, or something to do with renouncing the will, and sundry other bits of philosophical claptrap Minna couldn't understand. Then Mathilde would look back at her rich husband with wide eyes as if to say *Darling, we could have this all the time, our very own genius, creating the artworks of the future, right here at our back door! Don't you just love it?* And he – besotted with her oval face, rich brown hair, poetic leanings and complete lack of guile, wanting more than anything to make her happy – would nod his assent.

This infatuation was a problem, Minna reasoned, but a house was a house, and with her in Asyl and Otto in the mansion up the hill it would be surely be difficult for anything to happen. Still, she was nearly forty-eight, and there was temptation for Richard only a few flower beds away in the form of a beautiful other woman nearly twenty years Minna's junior. She would have to keep an eye on things, unlike that unfortunate business back in 1850 when her husband almost ran off to the Orient with the twenty-one-year-old Jessie Laussot hussy.

This time, Minna would be more vigilant. Richard's pants would stay firmly fastened unless he lowered them for his wife (never, these days) and he might even stop tinkering with his Ring of the Nibelung folly to write a smash hit that would make them some money. A nice comedy, perhaps, with real people in it, instead of gods and dwarfs.

Then he could damned well pay the rent.

Peps the King Charles spaniel gave his gasping bark at the sound of footsteps on the gravel path outside the front door.

'Ah! The Wagners are here!' said Mathilde Wesendonck as she fluttered into the room, her cheeks reddened by the dash through the rain. 'Richard – *welcome*. And you, Frau Wagner.' Minna did not fail to notice how different the two greetings sounded.

'My dear Mathilde, we have taken up residence ahead of you!' said Wagner, kissing her hand.

'Our new home won't be ready for a few months yet,' she said, blushing further, 'but I'll make a point of seeing you *every* day.' Wagner kissed her hand again, and Minna felt another of those pangs of jealousy.

'That's too kind of you, Frau Wesendonck, but we wouldn't wish to burden you with our company all the time, would we, Richard?' This was more of a prompt than a question.

Wagner would not be prompted.

'Frau Wesendonck's presence is essential to my peace of mind and the quality of my work,' he said. 'She is my Muse.' At this, Mathilde's flush extended all the way down her neck to the beginning of her décolletage.

She's your landlady, Minna thought.

Only the landlady.

~

Richard set up his writing table near one of the larger windows so that the view of the lake and distant mountains would inspire him. 'I must have beauty, splendour and light!' he insisted, a challenging requirement from someone who was penniless.

He set to work with discipline and speed, writing on vast pages of manuscript paper each morning. Best of all as far as Minna was concerned was that he looked to be moving on from the Nibelung project that had preoccupied him for years; it was now so enormous that only an opera house out of its mind could contemplate taking it on. She left that sort of sort of insanity to Richard himself when he said that the Ring would eventually require a theatre to be purpose-built for its production.

One morning he suggested this elephantine conceit might rest for a while. Other ideas were crowding in.

'I've started on a treatment for a new work called Parsifal,' he announced.

'Just the one opera?' Minna asked.

'Just the one.'

'Any gods or dwarfs?'

'Probably God himself, but there's a magician. Oh – and some flower maidens.'

'How delightful! It's a comedy then,' she said brightly.

'No.'

'Oh,' she said.

'That's not all. I've finally decided to start work on something else: a love story. It's been in the back of my mind ever since we met the Wesendoncks a few years ago. Now that we are here in Asyl it has become an impulse I can't ignore any more.'

'Richard, that sounds splendid!' said Minna, sensing that her husband was finally showing some awareness of public taste. 'People *adore* a love story! Who is the gorgeous couple?'

'Tristan and Iseult, from medieval times. She's a princess.'

'I love it! Do they end up happily ever after?'

'Possibly – but not in this world. He's killed by a sword.'

'And the princess?'

'Well, it's been an adulterous love, so she can't just go back to her husband. She sublimates herself.'

'Sublimates herself?'

'She is absorbed into the higher reality and renounces everything, including life.'

'Meaning . . . ?'

'She drops dead. Minna, my dear, you can't understand unless you've been there,' he said.

'I don't see why it should be so difficult, Richard,' she said. 'We've both been there as far as the adultery is concerned. It wouldn't have been all that helpful to me if I'd gone out and sublimated myself.'

'*Mathilde* understands, though,' said Richard, unable to conceal the reverential tone in his voice. 'We've discussed transcendental love at length, and she thinks I should start without delay. She has almost put the poem in my head.'

'I suppose she had to put it *somewhere*,' said Minna, without a trace of reverence.

And sure enough, within a couple of weeks Wagner announced that his Siegfried was now under a tree, and would stay there at least until the new Tristan story had been told. The massive sheaf of Ring manuscript was placed in an armoire and replaced by a clean sheet of writing paper.

He worked feverishly for almost a month, his brow shining with the heat of late summer. After lunch, he cleared his head by taking a walk through a forest near the estate, and then dashed across the Wesendonck lawn to meet Mathilde, waiting on a bench near a copse of trees, to read her that morning's work.

As he did so, she sat there looking at him in a way that Minna found deeply irritating whenever she contrived to peer at them unseen from a nearby hedge. Sometimes Mathilde would avert her gaze to the lake and exhale softly, all the while mouthing the words '*Yes*, Richard – yes, yes, *yes*.' If Minna had heard the same from behind a closed door she would have sworn that something less cerebral had taken place, but here was Frau Wesendonck in the open air, responding with something resembling post-coital gasps to the mere sound of Richard's words. God knows what she might do when she eventually heard the music.

In September, with the first trees beginning to turn, Richard said the poem was done. When Minna asked if perhaps *she* could hear the result, he announced that he would read it to an assembly of visitors.

'I don't receive a *private* rendition, Richard?' she said reproachfully.

'Mathilde has already assured me that the poetry is there,' he said. 'Now *Tristan* must be performed before an *audience*. You are to be a part of history, my dear.'

Minna attempted to console herself with this when the three couples retired to Asyl's small salon after dinner later that week. Joining the Wagners were the Wesendoncks, of course – Minna hoped that Mathilde would suppress her gasps in mixed company for the sake of propriety – and the Wagners' own houseguests, fresh from a honeymoon: young Hans von Bülow, a brilliant pianist and conductor who worshipped her husband, and the new Frau von Bülow.

Cosima was not only one of Franz Liszt's daughters, but seemed to have inherited an even larger version of her father's already significant nose. She was remarkably quiet for someone who should have been bubbling with a newlywed's enthusiasm, keeping her eyes averted from almost everyone except Richard, only to stammer something unintelligible and look away whenever he asked her a question.

Darkness closed in while Wagner intoned his poetry. Tristan and Isolde declared the night to be the only true home for their love. The glow of a single lamp in the darkness, the cadence of the author's voice as it rocked to the alliterations in the text, and the stillness outside punctuated only by the distant slush of water from the lake transported everyone back in time; Tristan lying dead on a Brittany shore, his lover standing alongside in an ecstatic trance.

After the final words:

To drown
To sink
Unconscious –
Supreme bliss!

... a silence fell over the company as they imagined Isolde falling lifeless onto Tristan's body.

Minna thought the whole thing was indecently passionate,

almost disgusting, and looked at the faces of the other women in the room.

Mathilde's expression had followed Isolde into the cosmos, her eyes closed, her mouth open. Cosima, on the other hand, burst into tears.

The whole thing was rather confusing.

Within days Wagner began writing the music. The notes flew onto the paper with such speed that Minna suspected the beginning of *Tristan*'s gestation went back much further than their arrival at Asyl.

'This idea isn't new to you, is it, Richard?' she said.

'I wrote to Liszt about it years ago,' he said. 'I've wanted to do a love story like this ever since I started reading Schopenhauer.'

'When was that?'

'Around the same time as meeting the Wesendoncks, I suppose.'

You mean around the same time you met her, Minna thought.

Now and then she heard him trying out some of the music on his piano, sometimes taking on a vocal line in his strange, hectoring voice. Minna had grown up listening to some beautiful parlour songs about love, but for the life of her, she couldn't hear much romance in whatever Richard was dreaming up. The music didn't seem to start anywhere, and it certainly didn't know where it was going. There wasn't the comfort of a tonal centre; none of the chords resolved in such a way that her ears could take a rest. She hoped that *Tristan and Isolde* would sound a bit happier later on, because nobody would pay money to go to a theatre and eavesdrop on this miserable affair.

Five months after moving in, Richard had stayed true to

his word and not paid a single franc in rent, so Minna could hardly complain about Mathilde's daily visits to his workroom for a progress report on the work. It was hard to tell what was going on behind his closed door – even with one's ear pressed very close to the keyhole – but she appeared to be urging him to continue along the strange path he was beating.

'Oh *Richard*, you make me feel it – right *here*,' she would murmur. 'I have written poetry to match. Please, take it.'

Minna took a discreet look at some of Frau Wesendonck's literary efforts strewn over the top of the piano when the pair had concluded one of their 'artistic' rendezvous. It was the usual nonsense full of angels, sunsets, crowns of leaves, dreams vanishing into the soul; if anything, even worse than Richard's opera. Closer inspection showed musical notation scribbled around the margins on some pages. *My God!* she thought, *he's actually toying with the idea of setting some of this to music.*

Otto was strangely mute during these early days in *Tristan*'s life. At first he was preoccupied with the move into Villa Wesendonck that August; but by November he had more urgent matters on his mind. His business was in trouble, and he needed to travel to the US to sort out the mess.

Richard Wagner prepared himself to step into the breach.

'Mathilde will be concerned about Otto, so we must make sure she is diverted,' he said to Minna at breakfast. Outside, their view of the lake was becoming less impeded by the falling leaves of autumn.

'You don't think you have diverted her enough?' said Minna. The former actress in her thought the archness in the delivery was a triumph.

'It's her birthday next month. I'm arranging to perform a setting of one of her poems with a small orchestra at the villa.'

'I thought we were here for you to compose for the benefit of *our* family, rather than someone else's.'

'My work will benefit,' Wagner said, once again placing himself at the centre of the discussion. 'The music in this setting of "Dreams" is a precursor to the duet between Tristan and Isolde in Act Two. If I can capture that sense of otherworldly love, then I'll know where to go when I arrive at that point in the drama.'

'Where are you now?'

'Still in Act One. Tristan and Isolde are just about to take the love potion. I'll play the sequence to Mathilde later this morning.'

Minna looked at Richard with a slight sense of relief. She should never have doubted that everything in his life was fodder for his work – even his emotional states. Was his obvious closeness to Mathilde inspiring his thoughts about Tristan? Or was it the other way around? She wondered if one even had to *be* in love in order to describe it. Perhaps one loved only when something inside gave the instruction for the door to be opened. Who on earth could love like Tristan and Isolde, anyway? By the sound of it, their level of passion had to be induced with a spiked drink.

If Richard *was* cultivating Mathilde's affection purely for the sake of his work, there was little for Minna to worry about. As soon as Isolde died in the opera, it was inevitable that Mathilde would 'die' too; she would be discarded, her usefulness as muse at an end. Richard would return to some normality in their married life.

Minna corrected herself with a start. *What* normality? There had never been anything 'normal' in more than twenty years together. How could there be, with someone like Richard Wagner? His mission in life was to be anything *but* normal, to be a sort of 'super' being, destined to re-establish music and drama as the salvation of Western thought. He literally burned with this ambition, the skin on his face blistering with erysipelas, his eyes too sensitive to light not generated by his own declared brilliance, his conversation only a vehicle for the expression of his ideas. To be involved with Richard was not to feel any sort of soft complicity; it was to be drawn into a bonfire of a unique mind. That was the most attractive thing about him; certainly not his small size, his profile with that beaky nose, those fanatical pale blue eyes, or the high forehead that parted the air in front of him like the prow of a ship so that his ideas could burn through the gap.

~

December 23rd was a clear winter day on the Wesendonck estate, and at seven o'clock in the morning the entrance hall of the villa was full of musicians. While Richard conducted, a violinist played the vocal part of *Dreams* in birthday homage to the poet.

Mathilde stood in the doorway of her bedroom, her face glowing with pleasure, as the strange harmonies floated up like incense from below.

Minna handed out sandwiches and coffee after the unorthodox performance. Everyone stood around admiring the sumptuous décor of the marble walls and tessellated floors in the hall and looked forward to meeting the beautiful young chatelaine of Villa Wesendonck when she would finally complete her toilette and come downstairs to join them.

The new music also attracted comment.

'I don't know what she's supposed to be singing about, but it certainly isn't about flowers in the spring,' said the horn player.

'Well, it's called "Dreams", isn't it?' noted another.

'Judging by what Herr Wagner has come up with, it's the sort of dream I'd definitely have if Frau Wesendonck could be in it,' whispered a portly violist.

'Definitely the whiff of a smoking loin,' giggled the bassoonist.

'I wonder what the husband thinks about it?' asked the horn player.

'What he doesn't know won't concern him,' said the violist. 'He's not even here.'

'More to the point – I wonder what the *wife* thinks about it?' said a violinist, indicating Minna across the room. '*She's* here.'

'*Gentlemen!*' Wagner's voice punctuated the gossip.

Mathilde descended the grand stairway of the hall to take Wagner's hand and be led into the circle of admirers. Several people applauded. Minna was not one of them.

'Please meet the inspiration for both "Dreams" and its bigger sibling, a magnificent music drama that I intend to complete next year. Madame,' he said, turning to face her, 'please accept the winter flower of "Dreams" for your Christmas tree. It is full of sweet honey, without the smallest bane.'

Mathilde nodded, her eyes moistening, and a few of the players applauded.

Leave the bane to me, Minna thought.

'Gentlemen, I propose a toast to Frau Wesendonck on her birthday, and of course to my wife. It is a fact that women are the music of life.'

There was a small silence, then a few dutiful chuckles.

'You know, I thought the composer of *Tannhäuser* might have come up with a better line than that,' said the bassoonist.

Otto Wesendonck returned home from New York the very next day, Christmas Eve, having sorted his business affairs to his satisfaction. Now it looked as if things needed to be fixed at home.

'What's going on?' he asked his wife. 'I go away for a month, and when I come back everything around here is changed. We have more servants, different mealtimes – even the heating has been altered.'

'Richard decided to take charge of things in your absence, dear,' explained Mathilde. 'He saw that our routine in the new house was still developing and had some ideas about improving our level of comfort.'

'Herr Wagner should be concerned only with the level of comfort in his *own* house,' said Wesendonck. 'And he should be amply comfortable by now in Asyl, given the amount of rent he owes us. If he wants to continue as a tenant, *that* should be his first priority rather than busying himself to ensure my wife is sufficiently warm at night.'

'Otto! I'm not sure that I like your inference.'

'Madame, *I* am sure that I dislike the stories I am beginning to hear around Zurich. The Wagners are here entirely by our indulgence. They need to show some respect for that, and restore some sense of propriety to the arrangement.'

'I assure you that the relationship I have with Richard is purely a meeting of minds,' said Mathilde, her heart racing. 'He is creating great art: a drama about transcendent love, infidelity, and the negation of will. He wishes to have me as a sounding board while he brings these ideas to life. That is all.'

'Well, that makes me feel a *whole* lot better,' said Otto. 'Madame, it is said that art imitates life. I trust that isn't the case here, but I also require Herr Wagner's assurance of it. Please have him come to see me without delay.'

'So be it, dear husband, but bear in mind it is *my* wish that the Wagners stay here until such time as Richard can complete his work. He always says that what is being achieved in the peace of Asyl is more important than the petty transactions of this world.'

'I don't mind respecting your wishes, Madame. But Herr Wagner needs to be reminded how much his current peace is reliant upon the success of *my* petty transactions.'

Wagner left for Paris the following week to let things cool down. By the time he was due to return, Minna had planted out the kitchen garden in readiness for spring, and Mathilde looked to be taking a keen linguistic interest in her handsome new Italian tutor, Signor de Sanctis, who preferred to teach only during afternoon teas or long drives. Minna could not help but make a comparison between the hothouse love of *Tristan* and the fickle infatuations coursing around the Wesendonck estate. Richard would be livid with jealousy. *Good.* The situation was not yet so reassuring that the frantic beating of her heart would calm down and allow her to sleep through the night.

Wagner swept back into Asyl, shrouded in the passion and

longing for darkness in *Tristan*'s second act now forming in his head. And the rail trip hadn't helped.

'What is *wrong* with people?' he lamented to Mathilde one evening as he sat in her salon on one of his so-called Twilight Man visits. 'I could see in their dead eyes that none of them was capable of negation of the will.'

'Richard, there is much to restore *here* before you concern yourself with strangers on a train,' she said, trying to be helpful. 'You honoured me with a birthday concert during Otto's absence. Now you should honour him the same way. His will is still far from positive as far as you are concerned.'

'Which of my works do you think he should hear?' Wagner asked.

'I think that Beethoven would be more favoured under the circumstances,' she said, not having the heart to tell him outright that Otto had refused to allow another note of Wagner's to be heard in the house – or that her tutor did not find Richard the man or composer at all to his taste. An aesthetics lecturer at Zurich's Polytechnic, Francesco had convinced her of his qualifications to make such a judgement over the course of a passionate afternoon tea some days earlier.

So it was the older German master's music that filled Villa Wesendonck during Holy Week. While the Allegretto from the Seventh Symphony was played, Minna watched Mathilde, who gazed at Francesco, and Otto switched his attention between Mathilde and Wagner. Richard looked at the score, aware of how much the A minor tonality in the music and its shuffling tread added to his growing sense of despondency. His muse still showed some interest in *Tristan*'s progress, but these days she appeared equally fascinated by conjugating Italian verbs with her tutor. When he was presented with an ivory baton at the end of the evening's concert all he wanted to do was beat time with it on de Sanctis' head.

A week later, he tried to explain himself.

'I have just finished the full score of *Tristan*'s first act, my angel,' he said to Mathilde. 'It is the greatest work I have ever done. The music passes directly into experience; it glows with new passion and arousal. But outside, everything else feels in decline, like the potential climax of a vital love has been reached.'

'Richard, you know you can't use *that* word within the walls of my house,' Mathilde said nervously, casting a glance at her Dante text on the table.

'If you feel it, why can't you *say* it?' he cried as quietly as he could. 'Why can't you *act* upon it? Why won't you renounce this world, as Tristan and Isolde do theirs?'

'And how do you propose I do that, Richard?'

'We leave our partners, leave this place, and marry each other.'

Months before, Mathilde would say only *yes* to his every pronouncement. Not now that the wall between *Tristan* and the world had been breached by a single proposition.

'That is impossible, Richard. Worse still, it would be sacrilege.'

Sacrilege? He was aghast that someone who had shown an almost erotic pleasure at the thought of her operatic incarnation being unfaithful to a husband should suddenly revert to such a bourgeois sentiment. This was no time to be ordinary; the world would excuse *any* consequence of Richard Wagner's love.

The salon door opened, and de Sanctis slid into the room, aware that he was interrupting something.

'Signora!' he said, with gratuitous theatricality. 'It is late, I know, but we have a pact tonight to finish our Dante – *sì*?'

Wagner looked at them both, and then left. That night, he and his wife lay awake in their separate rooms.

~

The next morning, Minna guessed there was something afoot in the way the gardener looked from side to side before starting to cross the kitchen garden in the direction of Villa Wesendonck, clutching a letter in his hand.

'Friedrich!' she called, attempting to sound as insouciant as possible.

He stopped, turning scarlet.

'Urgent delivery?' she said.

'Some music for Frau Wesendonck,' he said truthfully, embarrassed more at looking like a furtive messenger. 'Herr Wagner has already left for his daily walk.'

'I am going up to the Wesendoncks' anyway,' said Minna. 'Let me take it.'

He blushed further, but passed her the scroll without demur.

Minna opened it. Inside, several sheets of pencilled manuscript were furled around a letter. She saw that the music was the sketch of *Tristan*'s Prelude; there was no point in trying to make head or tail of it.

The letter was titled 'Morning Confession'. This was better. She was always interested in a confession not meant for her.

When she had finished reading, Minna resolved on two courses of action.

First, she would go indoors and take something for her heart.

Indeed, she might need to be looked at in a sanatorium some-where, because she didn't feel right at all.

Second, though, she would fulfil her husband's wish and deliver the letter to Mathilde Wesendonck.

~

'If I were any ordinary woman,' said Minna Wagner, 'I should take this letter to your husband.'

Mathilde sat at the reading table in her salon, the 'Morning Confession' trembling in her hands.

'Madame, I have never presumed you to be ordinary,' she replied with total insincerity. 'It is *my* duty to take this to him.'

Minna was too delighted by the discomfiture of her husband's 'muse' to consider the consequences of this scandal. Otto Wesendonck would hardly want the Wagners to continue as his tenants – especially when so much rent was still outstanding – and Mathilde was no longer in a position to argue their case; not when she had to explain phrases such as 'My prayer to you is Love!' or 'Take my entire soul!'

It was amazing how such a genius could be so stupid. Richard had insisted for months that nothing had 'happened' between him and Mathilde; meaning physical intimacy, she supposed.

But an opera was taking shape on the page describing a love so intense that nobody would get out alive. Surely it was no accident that Richard had conceived the subject so soon after meeting Mathilde Wesendonck, already aware of her feelings for him. She became Isolde, the opera would be the love potion, and it followed that he, Richard, became Tristan. If this sub-urban, commonplace mutual infatuation on a Zurich lakeside were truly unconsummated, then all the better; the sheer tension of the situation served as *Tristan*'s source material.

Minna felt her hands balling into fists. *Oh yes, something had 'happened' all right*, she thought. It didn't matter whether Mathilde Wesendonck had opened her legs for Richard or not. There was plenty of sex in the air around Asyl, and it didn't involve herself or Otto. The musky smell of it was seeping out from the pages of that damned opera score.

It was a strange scene that met Richard upon his return from the daily forest walk.

The Wesendoncks' carriage was being loaded with what looked to be hastily packed luggage, more than required for a short trip. Mathilde was already seated for departure, her face deathly white. Otto, talking to the driver, turned to greet Wagner with a very strange smile on his face.

Wagner continued down the path, through the kitchen garden into Asyl's entrance hall. He thought he could hear music, and sure enough Minna was humming loudly when she emerged from the door to her bedroom. She looked radiantly happy.

'Richard!' she said, almost squealing with delight. 'How was your walk?'

'Minna?' he said, struggling to make sense of it.

'You've seen the Wesendoncks, then? It's very exciting. They've decided to go on a long trip to Italy.'

'*Italy*? What . . . ?'

'You know that Frau Wesendonck has been studying hard with her tutor? I think Otto decided to put her new knowledge to the test.'

'W-when did . . . ?'

'It's all happened only this morning. I suppose the Wesendoncks thought it the best thing to do once we all read your letter.'

'M-my . . . ?'

'*You* know, my dear – your "Morning Confession". And a very touching confession it is, too. Mathilde thought it was so beautiful, she just had to pass it around.'

Richard detected the rising note of sarcasm in Minna's voice, and his bewilderment turned to anger. It was inconceivable that Mathilde had betrayed their trust.

'What have you done, Minna? You must be aware that this could have very . . . *unpleasant* consequences.'

'But Richard, *what* unpleasantness?' said Minna. 'You've abandoned that Ring nonsense to write a more saleable love story. The Wesendoncks are taking a long holiday that Mathilde looks as if she needs, poor little pale thing.' Her words almost turned into a snarl. 'And both Herr Wesendonck and I *get our spouses back*. What we've had here has simply been a minor love affair. A bit of space for all concerned will calm everything down.'

Wagner turned cold at what he perceived as the final revelation of Minna's mediocrity. How could she possibly know what was required for the creation of great art? Minna was fretting about the pointless sanctity of people's reputations while he was focussed on something altogether greater: a musical form of greater unity and clarity than anything that had come before.

He decided that if *Tristan* was to continue to be realised – and it *must* – she could not be a party to it.

'I cannot vouch for Otto, but as far as *this* marriage is

concerned, you will *not* be getting your spouse back. It is probable we will have to leave this place because of your actions this morning. If that is so, you and I will no longer live together, madame.'

Minna started. She had expected Richard to capitulate once the futility of his attachment to Mathilde was explained, or whenever her role as *Tristan*'s muse expired with the completion of the opera. Indeed, Mathilde had started to drift away into a new nirvana of Italian lessons, abandoning Richard's requirements ahead of schedule and reducing him to the authorship of this morning's embarrassing, lovelorn document.

For heaven's sake, they had even spoken of late about the idea of adopting to compensate for their childless marriage. And now – *this*?

She took his hand and covered it with kisses.

'My dear Richard, if we were to separate it would only lend credence to the silly rumours that will make their way around town. Neither of us could possibly stay if the other disappeared. You talk about the stability that Asyl has brought to us, that it is a haven for your work. How would you continue with your *Tristan* if we again become homeless?'

Minna went on like this, her voice eventually giving way to gentle sobs. Wagner paid no attention as he looked at the lake through the window behind her. The proximity of water was such a balm, so primal, so womblike. And the harmonies of the songs he had composed for Mathilde came back to him with a deeper intensity, showing him in a flash the tone of the love dialogue in Act Two of what he knew would be his masterpiece. All he needed was a new space in which to work – space, silence, water – where Tristan and Isolde could be led to their inevitable, sublime fates.

Mathilde must now join Minna on the fringes of his emotional life. He would permit some correspondence, certainly; the Wesendonck money might still be useful to him in the future.

He decided to leave Asyl behind and travel south, following the water. Venice perhaps, a big room overlooking the Grand Canal. Some large red drapes on the walls. He would have to find someone for some cash. Liszt had been good for a touch or three in the past.

Once he was installed to his satisfaction, Richard could return to his score and kill someone.

POSTSCRIPT

Wagner left Minna behind in August 1858, travelling first to Venice and then Lucerne, where he completed *Tristan and Isolde* the following year. Minna disposed of their household effects in a public garage sale and ended up in Dresden, where she died from a heart attack in 1866. She and Wagner never lived together again.

Wagner began an affair with Cosima von Bülow and the couple had three children before her divorce was granted in 1870. In the meantime, her publicly cuckolded husband Hans von Bülow conducted the premiere of *Tristan* in Munich in 1865. The Wesendoncks did not attend.

Tristan and Isolde is widely considered to be the most influential work of Western art music ever written.

Scandal Goes West

Being the soprano in an opera by married playboy Giacomo Puccini was a dangerous business. All of them come to an unhappy end in his most successful works – excepting one, whose creation on the page overlapped a scandal of alleged adultery and suicide that grabbed the world's attention and virtually destroyed a marriage.

~'

'I am a mighty hunter of wild fowl, operatic librettos and attractive women.'

Giacomo Puccini (1858–1924)

OCTOBER 1907

The knock at the door was unexpected.

Seated at the piano, Giacomo Puccini had been watching the trail of smoke from the end of his cigarette, waiting for its ascent to give him a sign. If it passed the top of his head, the soprano would sing a G natural. Any further – perhaps to the bottom of the chandelier – and she would rise to a B flat.

Now his concentration was broken. *Dammit*, he thought, clicking the fingers of his right hand. *This is a Viennese luxury hotel, for God's sake! Don't they respect the privacy of the creative process?*

'*Sì?*' he said aloud, trusting that his Italian mixed with the note of annoyance on a gruff E natural would discourage the usual chambermaid from entering.

The voice at the door was not a woman's.

'Maestro? *Permesso?*' It was young, with a local accent.

Probably a hotel valet, the famous composer thought. He might have a letter. Perhaps another baleful one from Elvira. Then again, it might be from someone else; a message that would be far more exciting to read.

He pressed his thick dark hair close to the sides of his head and checked his tie before opening the door, right hand already outstretched for details of an assignation.

There was no letter, and no valet.

Instead, two people he guessed to be brother and sister stood before him. The young man looked up at him expectantly, while the young woman stared at her brother with a look of distaste on her face, as if she had just stepped in something. *She's a feisty one*, the older man deduced. He would have appraised her even more carefully had not the pair's anointed spokesperson piped up.

'Signor Puccini, forgive this intrusion. We told the reception downstairs that you had invited us for an audition.'

'That was my first question,' said Puccini. 'Here's the next.

How did you know I was here in Vienna?'

'When the world's most famous living opera composer comes to the world's most musical city to oversee a production of *Madama Butterfly*, *everyone* knows.'

The composer stroked his carefully cropped moustache. The young man had a point, but Puccini would not be flattered. He decided to harden his voice with more diaphragm support and a switch to the same high baritonal range his Baron Scarpia used when being sardonic in *Tosca*.

'Nevertheless, this *is* an intrusion. What is it you both want?'

'Just as we said. We'd like to audition. At least, I ask you to hear my sister.'

'Young man, this is pointless. I don't need to audition aspiring singers now. The production of *Butterfly* is underway.'

'We know that trying to see you under normal circumstances would have been impossible. We've travelled far for this. If you could give us just a few minutes, I hope you'll agree your time hasn't been wasted.'

The young woman muttered something to her brother in a dialect Puccini would never understand, glancing at the composer as she did so. It sounded like an angry instruction to drop the whole idea. No docility there, he observed. Perhaps she *was* a singer after all; much more a Tosca than a Mimi. What a little Austrian garden she would be.

'I'm trying to start my new opera,' he said, remembering the vapour trails from his cigarette, the notes from Minnie's aria now dispersed across the ceiling. 'Come in for a moment, and I'll take some details about your sister. We can arrange an audition for another time.'

'*Thank you*, maestro – thank you,' said the young man, motioning to his sister to enter. Puccini spun on his heels and walked elegantly towards the adjoining bedroom to find pen, paper and another cigarette, unaware of the exchange of whispers behind him.

Once inside, opening and closing the drawers of his bureau, he did not hear the discreet click of a closing door, or the rustle of cotton.

When Puccini returned to the spacious living area graced with the grand piano brought in specifically to suit the purposes of a famous musician, the young man had gone.

His sister remained behind, standing in front of a gilt mirror above the unused fireplace.

All her clothing was bunched on the floor next to her feet.

Ever the gentleman, Puccini looked at the mirror. The plaits at the back of her head were almost certainly an authentic rural decoration, he thought.

'Herr Puccini,' she said in a tone of voice that at last drew his attention to her face. 'I hope I can convince you that I'm deserving of any part you are able to offer me.'

The line was obviously rehearsed, and Puccini hoped the singing would be too – if that was what she did.

He reflected that the lovers in *La bohème* went from first meeting to proposition in little more than fifteen minutes in Act One. Rodolfo tells Mimi he is a poor poet with the soul of a millionaire, and she replies that she makes artificial flowers. Soon, he hints at what might happen afterwards if they go to the local bar that night. Puccini thought such a seduction was faster than anything humanly possible, but here was a naked young woman to prove him wrong. Opera was implausible; life even more so.

'We'll discuss *parts* shortly,' he said, sitting at the piano. 'First, though, I must know what you can do. *Vieni qui* – stand next to me. Sing an arpeggio on this note.' He placed his hand on her bare abdomen, stroking with outstretched fingers. 'I want to feel you support the voice.'

Afterwards, when the aspiring diva had returned to her waiting brother with a vow of secrecy given in return for vague assurances of a possible understudy role sometime in the future, Puccini buttoned his trousers, the sound of her coital cries still reverberating in his mind. He had expected something more operatic at the peak of their encounter, something that would really bring down the house. Instead, the young lady had barely ventured above a pianissimo, her top note only just an A flat. His initial impression had been wrong: she was more a Mimi than a Tosca.

While every opera composer tried to express character by choosing a certain sequence of notes for the voice, in Puccini's considerable experience nothing was more revealing of a woman's true nature than the sounds she made when all inhibitions had been abandoned, singing at its purest and most primal. Once the notes were learned, the effect would always ring true, even if the emotion was faked. Many onstage careers were built on such artifice. In that respect, sex *was* opera.

One year later

In the five years she had been working at Villa Puccini, ever since Signor Puccini's terrible car accident, Doria Manfredi had never heard anything like it. The maestro's stepdaughter was either in pain, or was asking a question over and over without receiving an answer.

Doria stood outside the room as the sounds of distress grew louder. 'Signora?' she ventured.

There was no response, and with both of her employers out of the house, she had to investigate. She opened the door as quietly as she could.

There was Fosca, looking for all the world like a wheelbarrow with her haunches raised at the edge of the bed, her arms extended backwards like a pair of handles. Standing behind her crouched form, grasping those handles and pushing the wheelbarrow more with his hips than his elbows, causing all the commotion as he did so, was the Puccinis' houseguest, Signor Civinini, who was supposed to be working on the libretto for the maestro's next opera, set in America's Wild West.

Doria doubted that Fosca's husband, Signor Leonardi, would approve. She brought a hand to her throat.

'*Scusi, scusi,*' she stammered, backing out of the room.

The couple only became aware of the intrusion as the door clicked shut. Fosca lifted her face from the pillow.

'Shit,' she said.

'What do we do?' said Civinini. 'If the maid says something, you're in disgrace and I lose a great job writing about cowboys.'

'We're going to have to discredit her before she discredits *us*,' said Fosca, who was bored with her husband anyway. 'I'll have a word with Mamma. She tends to suspect every woman within a ten-mile radius of the house. With good reason, I should add.'

'You'd better go right away.'

'There's nobody at home until dinnertime. And we haven't finished yet,' she said, reaching back.

~

'I need to talk to you about Papa,' Fosca said after dinner. Puccini wasn't her biological father, but she had known him since she was five, when the handsome young musician used to come around to give her mother piano lessons while her actual father was travelling away for work.

Elvira sighed, her mouth assuming its customary grimace.

'Don't expect me to be surprised, Fosca,' she said. 'I presume that once again, somewhere on his travels, he has found himself another *little garden?*'

'Little garden' was her husband's euphemism for whichever lover happened to be waiting back at the hotel while he supervised foreign productions of his works.

Not that she was supposed to know, of course. He would always insist that the work gave him no time for such things. In any case, didn't he love her enough to endure the scandal of their elopement more than twenty years earlier, when he whisked her away from her husband and family in Lucca to a life of notoriety, indignant landladies and backstage whispers? Hadn't he waited nearly twenty years for her first husband to die so that the way was clear for them to at last assume the respectability of their own marriage? And didn't she now enjoy the trappings of wealth and celebrity: devoted domestics like young Doria, one of the first cars in Italy, and the beautiful Villa Puccini, built on a spectacular lakeside plot in the country and decorated to their taste?

Torre del Lago. A village in the sticks. A place where her husband could go and shoot whichever unfortunate animal crawled into or flew over the estate and Lake Massaciuccoli. She hated it. It was all very well for Giacomo to sit in silence all day waiting for a passing bird to annihilate, or a passing tune to capture. What was *she* supposed to do in the meantime?

Milan beckoned, with restaurants, soirées, and endless compliments to Signora Puccini. They had money from performance royalties pouring in like rain. Why not live there, or in some other glamorous city?

Giacomo would not hear of it. 'I hate pavements,' he said.

Then there were the damned cars. Theirs was the first car in the village, followed by the first car *accident*, skidding through a bend in the road on a foggy night when the chauffeur lost control, landing upside down at the bottom of a ditch. She and their son Tonio were lucky, suffering only from shock. Giacomo broke his leg. All of Italy was riveted by the news. The King sent a get-well card.

At least the setback kept Giacomo at home for several months. Hobbling around on two walking sticks, wincing with the pain, he couldn't get back to work on the almost illegible manuscript of *Madama Butterfly* lying open at the piano. He also couldn't rush off to continue his affair with that Corinna girl he'd picked up in Turin three years before.

Elvira had got wind of that one when the pair was spotted in the café at the Pisa train station. She found out about most of his 'little gardens' by being vigilant; finding a stray letter, receiving an eyewitness report from a family friend. Sometimes he would slip off for an assignation even when Elvira was travelling with him. She even tried to medicate her husband into a state of morality with bromides in his coffee and camphor in his trouser pockets – anything to keep his pecker down.

It was a fruitless struggle against Nature; at least, Puccini's nature.

Thank heavens for the loyalty of servants like Doria, Elvira thought. Little Doria, who had been at the Villa Puccini ever since the accident in 1903, when she came to them as a callow teenager. She had been so sweet to Giacomo during his convalescence, bringing him his five meals a day, and remained a fixture in the running of the household while so many others had come and gone. To the Puccinis, Doria was a treasure; they called her so. They had watched her grow up.

'It's about Doria,' Fosca said.

~

The news was shattering. If Puccini had been setting Fosca's revelation to music in an opera, there would have been a stark line played in unison by the whole orchestra, or a chord sequence on a tritone like that at the beginning of *Tosca*.

The gestures of real life could never compare to the drama of theatre. The best he could do was to slam the butt of his unloaded gun into the floor with a loud cracking sound.

His next spluttered word emerged in an unfortunate head voice.

'What?' *Not effective*, he thought. *If this was a libretto, I'd send it back to Civinini.*

'I have thrown Doria out of this house and our service, Giacomo,' said Elvira, her grimace now a sneer. 'She is lucky I did not do worse.'

'Why?' (*Monosyllables don't convey sufficient outrage. Use cymbals.*)

'*You know why!*' she yelled. He *didn't* know why, yet had to admit that the accusation was impressive in its delivery.

There was a pause. (*String tremolo here. Crescendo leading to . . .*)

'*Gardens!*' she spat out.

Giacomo was confused. Why didn't Elvira fire the gardener? She *had* fired the gardener just a few days before, in fact. And the cook.

'Little gardens,' she said more softly. 'You have brought your little garden under this roof.'

Puccini continued to unwind his scarf, trying to make sense of this. He had just returned from shooting; it was a cold morning.

'You and Doria are having an affair,' Elvira continued.

'Me – and *Doria*?' He realised instantly that mere incredulity was never an effective retort.

'There is no point in denying it, Giacomo. You have been *seen* together.'

'Elvira, when someone has worked in one's house for six years, being seen together is somewhat inevitable.'

'I mean – *together*. You have been observed *in flagrante*.'

Even the imaginary orchestra fell quiet. Puccini's mouth fell open. The intake of fresh air reminded him that he needed a cigarette. Probably his fifteenth for the day.

Elvira's jealousy, while not unwarranted, had long since grown from an irritant to a matter of bemused discussion between Puccini and his friends. 'She gets on my nerves, Giacomo!' his former librettist Illica had said one day as they worked on the previous hits *La bohème*, *Tosca* and *Butterfly*. Everyone noticed that the composer occasionally smelled as if he had been embalmed, thanks to the bizarre aroma wafting from his pants. More than once, Puccini had been aware of a figure dressed in his own clothes observing him in the street; the distinctive waistcoats of his taste not quite concealing the familiar bustline that had piqued his interest twenty years before during piano lessons with his friend's wife.

At least these actions had a point; Elvira was following a real trail. Puccini was a naughty boy, and he knew it. He bragged about it.

This time was different. This time Elvira was being delusional, even psychotic. It was impossible that Elvira, or anyone, had seen anything at all. There was nothing to see.

Doria? He was writing an opera with his most complex female central character yet. How would Doria ever show up in *any* opera of his, except as some meek and simple servant, bless her?

He knew that the meek *were* blessed, of course, just as the Good Book said. That was how Mimi and Butterfly started out in his works; Mimi, the shy, sickly seamstress living in poverty, and Cio-Cio-san, the fifteen-year-old offered as a bride of convenience to a visiting American lieutenant.

Yet those two had qualities he did not sense in Doria: an underlying strength of character – as Mimi must have had to

cope in big-city Paris, where life among the young bohemians would have toughened her moral code – and an integrity
that saw the two through personal crises; in Butterfly's case,
choosing death over dishonour. Puccini could not put Doria in
that class.

The woman he needed right now was one who could help
him find a way into the character of Minnie for his new work.
Long ago, it had been Elvira who showed him the persona of
Manon Lescaut in his first major success. Elvira was not Minnie,
however; neither was Doria.

Who, then? Puccini suspected he had found someone.
Looks had been exchanged; there was something he recog-
nised in the smile. She was nearby. In that and other respects,
Doria had already proved useful. Elvira's aim was awry. Instead
of hitting the target, she had shot the messenger.

*In a small place like Torre del Lago, the wound will only be skin-
deep, surely?*

~

Puccini found her in the street, not far from the Chalet Emilio,
the local bar that was his intended destination. Good – she
could finish the mission.

'*Doria* – Doria,' he said, trying to restrain her.

She glanced at him, clearly terrified.

'Signor Puccini ... I cannot ... I cannot speak with you here.'

'Doria, I just want to tell you how sorry I am. You and I both
know how wrong my wife is about this.'

'Maestro, it's no longer about what *we* think. I'm scared
about how this may look to others.'

'Others won't know. It's in both your and the Puccini family's interests to keep this unfortunate situation to ourselves.'

'We're a small town, signor. Everyone knows everyone else's business. How can people *not* know? My family don't understand.'

'Doria, we can help you find another employer. I'll say and write the most complimentary things about your character. They're the truth.'

'Signor, the truth no longer matters. The signora's made sure of it. People are interested only in the worst that can be said of others.' Tears welled in her eyes.

Puccini placed one hand on her shoulder to steady the onset of grief. With his other he dipped into his fragrant trouser pocket and withdrew an envelope.

'In the meantime, dear Doria, can you take this? You know where it must go.'

She looked at him again, puzzled.

'Signor, are you joking? I can't take any further part in this. It'll destroy me. Perhaps it already has. People mustn't see us together.' She forced the envelope back into his grasp.

'Doria, things may be easier this way. At least we're away from the prying eyes of my house.'

'WHORE!' The voice bellowed from the other side of the street. Passers-by stopped dead.

A figure in men's clothing strode towards them. The scene had the same sense of dire coincidence as a tawdry Act Two finale. This was the melodramatic dénouement of early Verdi; not Puccini.

Except it was the chatelaine of the Villa Puccini whose

fantasy had now been vindicated by the wrong impression.

'What's that in your hand, Giacomo?' She laughed. 'A *love* letter?'

At last Elvira was correct, but only for a single sentence. Puccini folded the envelope carefully and returned it to his pocket.

'It must be a chore to have to write everything down now instead of whispering to each other in bed,' she continued.

Doria's face turned white; she looked as if she was about to faint. An onlooker ran into the bar.

'I only wanted to thank Doria for her years of service ...' Puccini began.

'Surely you have thanked her enough? The same gratitude you have shown to so many others over the years,' said Elvira.

'Signora, this is not a conversation that should take place in the street,' Puccini said in an undertone.

'This conversation *belongs* in the street, as does your little servant here,' said Elvira, raising her voice. 'She is a filthy whore and a tart.'

She turned to address the growing number of spectators who had formed a circle around them.

'This *treasure* of the village is a tramp who ran after my husband and seduced him in my own home. I warn *anyone* here who thinks of employing her that your home is just as unsafe. She has been thrown out of mine, and as surely as there is a Christ and a Madonna I will drown her in the lake if I ever see her in Torre del Lago again.'

Doria Manfredi began to retch, her legs giving way. A woman burst through the door of the Chalet Emilio and elbowed her way through the crowd in time to catch the sagging figure.

'Come with me, cousin,' she said. Puccini looked fixedly at the newcomer, who threw a look of hot steel at Elvira.

'*Signora* Puccini,' she said with sarcastic deference, 'you pretend to live like the highest in our village, but you speak like the lowest. How little you deserve your good fortune.' She cast a peculiar look at Giacomo and then returned to his wife. 'I would appreciate you moving along. It doesn't look good for us to have *scum* near the door. Please let us through, everyone.'

She half-carried the younger woman away, assisted by a man who also emerged from the bar's entrance, probably a customer.

What a superb rejoinder, what a magnificently contemptuous toss of the head, Puccini thought with something close to pride, even as he tried to comprehend the degree of humiliation that had just descended upon his family. The whole scene had been so *operatic*.

He straightened himself, which together with a particularly dapper wardrobe choice that morning and freshly cropped moustache – gave him a look of elegant stoicism, and took his wife's arm.

'Come, signora,' he said. 'I think we should take you home and get you out of my clothes.'

The next day, a letter arrived from Doria's brother, Rodolfo. 'Signor Puccini,' it said. 'You have brought dishonour to my sister and our family, and we are grateful to your poor wife for bringing this to our attention. Doria denies everything. We know she is only doing this to try and protect you. Do not think you are protected. Be warned: I would happily kill you for this. The next time you go out shooting you must be very careful.'

Puccini lurched up from his desk, suddenly aware of the twinge in his injured leg, and left his study. He felt strangely impotent as he stood in the hall, clutching the sheet of paper. Did one *file* such a thing? Throwing it away wouldn't dissolve its power.

Fosca emerged from the dining room in the company of Civinini. *He'll never finish* La fanciulla del West *if she keeps distracting him*, Puccini thought, still unaware of the nature of the distraction.

'Fosca, someone is threatening to kill me over this absurd business with Doria,' he said. 'People actually *believe* the evil things your mother is saying.'

'We *all* do, signor,' she said, coldly. 'Everybody knows what you are like. Are you not a *mighty hunter*? This time you have been shooting too much on your own estate.'

So, there was no one to take his part, thought Puccini. Soon the newspapers would join the chorus of opprobrium. What an irony; that he should emerge almost scot-free from a long list of real infidelities over the years, only to be scuppered by a single baseless accusation. Heaven knew he was not perfect, but Italian society usually cut its menfolk some slack in such matters. He was rich and celebrated, handsome and talented; an aristocrat in all but birthright. Puccini couldn't think of a single aristocrat of his acquaintance who *didn't* have a mistress or two. Even if he *had* taken Doria as a lover, it wouldn't be the first time the lord of the manor had rung downstairs for service.

Now Elvira had convincingly portrayed herself as the wronged party, with he and Doria as the villains. It was all becoming too much like a Puccini opera, in which the innocent women bore the brunt of punishment by cruel circumstance. Manon

Lescaut, Mimi, Floria Tosca, Cio-Cio-san – none of them ended their operas alive.

Puccini trusted there would come a point when Life stopped imitating Art.

In the meantime, he would take the heat out of the situation by removing himself from it. He decided to go to Rome for some peace, a hotel room and a piano. His Minnie was taking on real flesh and blood, her music now surging in his mind, the setting of the Wild West bar brimming with orchestral colour.

The day after he checked in, a telegram arrived from Torre del Lago.

Doria had poisoned herself. Several days later, she was dead.

~

'Three tablets of corrosive sublimate,' said the doctor, a family friend who had stood as witness to Giacomo and Elvira's marriage. 'Mercury poisoning, in other words. It would have been an agonising death. She regretted it immediately, but it was too late. The family says she insisted to the end you weren't to be blamed.'

'What happens now?' asked Puccini.

'The local court has demanded an autopsy. There's a strong rumour in the village that Doria had an abortion, and every finger in Torre del Lago is pointed at you.'

'Oh, my God. It can't happen soon enough, then. This tragic opera must end. Where is Elvira?' Not that he cared.

'Milan. She's doubtless preparing to return in triumph when the autopsy results are made known.'

Elvira would not return so soon. Torre del Lago was agog

with the news delivered to the courts from the surgeon's table.

Doria had died *virgo intacta*. A virgin.

It was all the customers talked about at the Chalet Emilio that evening. Giulia Manfredi noted the hypocrisy of such intimate detail, something of concern only to her immediate family, bringing a sigh of relief to an entire village. Up until then the bar had been a place of strained silence, averted eyes, surreptitious pointing, an odour of scandal enveloping her family, the sour sense of judgement having been passed. Many regulars simply stayed away.

Now they came back, eager to kiss her on both cheeks, order more drinks than usual, offering the condolences over the death of her cousin that had been withheld. Doria – and by extension her family – were now vindicated.

Giulia's face relaxed into the round, full-lipped smile that captivated everybody. She bantered and teased her regulars just as in happier days, her voice caramel in tone, her dark brown eyes beneath a fringe of tousled hair charming every object of their attention.

The muddle of public opinion now gave way to a clear collective anger, trained on a single target.

'Defamation and slander leading to suicide,' said Puccini's lawyer on the phone. 'The Manfredis want Elvira's blood, and while they're at it, take both of you to the cleaners.'

It was no surprise. Puccini exhaled cigarette smoke and watched the cloud collect at the ceiling, his yellow-tipped fingers tapping on a clean sheet of manuscript paper.

'Shit. The Manfredis can't be bought off?'

'Not right now they can't. They know what an iron-clad case

they have; eyewitnesses queueing around the block, and probably a few handwritten surprises to come from Doria herself.'

Puccini tightened his lips.

'What does Elvira say?'

'She says it's all your fault, and that God will call you to account very soon unless you confess your guilt.'

'The bitch is mad. If she had any heart left she would feel remorse. Tell her not to bother coming back.' Puccini slammed down the receiver.

It was bad enough that he couldn't sleep without Doria's face constantly in his mind's eye; not the impassive features of the Doria he knew, but another face, the mouth twisted in agony, the cheeks hollowed, her eyes rolling upward with delirium as the poison slowly ate away at her guts.

Was she unable to cope with the shame caused by Elvira's public tirade? Her family thought so.

Then there were her alleged final words: *'Tell the maestro he is not to blame for this . . .'*

It was a strange remark.

Puccini already knew they were both innocent of Elvira's charges. He had no need of reassurance.

Was it said to exculpate him in the eyes of her family? Surely not; she would have known that the investigations surrounding her death would prove the accusations were baseless, just as had happened.

Puccini had *needed* Doria – but not in the way Elvira believed.

Could it be her suicide was meant to *protect* him? Not quite. Doria had sacrificed herself to preserve honour; not hers, and not Giacomo's.

Doria was protecting someone else.

Of *course* she was, Puccini realised. In Torre del Lago, blood was thicker than water.

This time Puccini would not write. No other courier could be trusted.

Elvira wasn't coming back any time soon. He would make a personal call on Giulia Manfredi.

His opera depended upon it.

~

He looked overdressed when he arrived at the bar, and the hair that had noticeably greyed in the past couple of months had the stylish signature of a Milanese barber. The eyes possessed an almost dreamy expression, regarding everyone from beneath hooded lids. He greeted Signora Manfredi with quiet politeness and lit a cigarette.

Everyone accepted the man could do with a drink after the events of the past week. But surely there was no shortage of liquor at the Villa Puccini? He must be worth a fortune.

Some were more understanding. Why would Signor Puccini want to spend time with *that woman* in the house? Especially when she was about to be hauled off to court. A murderess in all but deed. She may as well have administered the poison.

Puccini felt the swirl of opinion around him, but remained unperturbed. It helped him to understand the character of Dick Johnson in *La fanciulla del West* (or *The Girl of the Golden West*), a man with a secret who decides to clean up his act when he falls in love with Minnie, the gun-toting, feisty woman who runs the local saloon.

He sings about his love near the end of the opera, when he is caught and about to be hanged as a thief. Rather than have her devastated by the news, he asks that she instead be told he was freed and has gone to seek a better life.

Puccini already had that tune in his head. He could hear Caruso's voice rising to the B flat twice during the aria, Toscanini suspending the huge orchestra while the tenor made a meal of that high note, and the sobbing and yelling of the Metropolitan Opera audience when it was over.

For the first time, Puccini wouldn't kill his lead soprano character. Minnie loves in return. Dick is saved and redeemed by that love when the opera ends, and the two ride together out of California and the Sierra Mountains to a new life, leaving behind her heartbroken bar crowd. Who would pour their drinks now?

It grew late, and the Chalet Emilio regulars left in their usual haze, unsure of who might have lingered.

Giulia extinguished the lamps, throwing the bar into darkness, and took her last remaining customer upstairs. The untended fire was no match for the chill of January, so there was no time for caresses before bed. Besides, she was impatient to get started. There had been too much unsatisfying correspondence.

The coupling was honest and brief, just like Giulia's conversation. Puccini noted that as a diabetic of fifty he was not the man of twenty-five who had astonished Elvira so long ago; the tempo had slowed to a comfortable andante. In music, the climax always carries more weight after a slow build. Giulia's cry when it came was just as impressive. In it, Puccini divined the code that he would take back to the bare manuscript sheets on his desk.

Now the music could arrive in all its detail. He had his *Fanciulla*.

POSTSCRIPT

Elvira Puccini claimed to be too ill to attend her trial, which made international news. In absentia, she was convicted of slander, defamation and menaces and sentenced to five months and five days in prison. She was spared the ignominy of serving time when her husband reached an out-of-court settlement with the Manfredis for a massive 12,000 lire in return for their withdrawal of all charges.

The couple were reunited in a holiday spa town later in 1909 and lived together uneasily for the rest of Puccini's life. He died while receiving treatment for an inoperable throat cancer in November 1924, leaving behind an unfinished opera, *Turandot*. One of its main characters is a slave girl, Liù, who kills herself rather than betray her employer's secret.

Giulia Manfredi gave birth to a son in June 1923 and christened him Antonio (the same name as Puccini's son by Elvira, named after the composer's grandfather), who was raised in Pisa with the initial assistance of 1,000 lire a month in maintenance from an anonymous donor. The money stopped abruptly in December 1924.

Antonio Manfredi died in 1988 without having discovered the identity of his father. Among the effects left to his daughter was an old suitcase. When opened years later, its contents included letters and signed photographs to Giulia Manfredi from Giacomo Puccini.

Mazurka in a
Teaspoon

The affair of Chopin and George Sand has long been
the stuff of legend. It's probable that the Pole would
neither have composed as much, nor lived as long,
without Sand's intellectual and material support.
Detail about the beginning of their relationship is
largely a matter of speculation, but all those who knew
them both agreed on one thing: it took a brave person
to step onto a sexual battlefield littered with so
many corpses.

~

*'Man is never always happy, and very often only a brief period of
happiness is granted him in this world.'*

Frédéric Chopin (1810–1849)

Paris, 24 October 1836

George looked at the pale face and thought it was the most beautiful she had ever seen: blue-grey eyes, a gaze at once dreamy and possessed, burnt blond hair cascading to his shoulders. She wanted to cradle that face between her hands, cover it with kisses.

It belonged to the exotic pianist from Poland, Frédéric Chopin, and George Sand had waited a long time to see it and hear some of his music praised by so many. She had pestered her friend Franz about making an introduction.

'That's not as easy as you think,' said the tall Hungarian piano virtuoso, flicking his mane of hair back behind his shoulders. 'One day he'll hide in his room and declare life is all over, and the same night he'll caper and mimic at a society party until the small hours. Fred only likes who he knows. Makes it hard for strangers, and difficult to forge introductions. If you *really* want to meet him, George, let's just throw a party. Now that Marie and I are back from our time in Switzerland, we'll call it a housewarming. Just be careful. Fred's not the strongest of men. We don't want you killing him and leaving his broken heart to be dissected by the feuilletons, like all the others they say you've left behind.'

'Franzi! Never believe what you read,' said George, knocking the ash from her thin cigar, her enormous brown eyes blinking with mock indignation. It was an ironic remark, coming from one of the most celebrated and notorious writers of the time, the most famous woman in France, whose novels dripped with autobiographical detail. The real-life affairs of George Sand were the fodder of much salon gossip.

The soirée took place at the Hôtel de France on the rue Laffitte in rooms George shared with Franz Liszt, his mistress the Countess d'Agoult, and their baby daughter, Blandine. George and Marie were of like mind, independent spirits who had managed their escapes from marriages of convenience with the consolations of new lovers.

As evening fell, the room was full of conversation George found instructive: news on the latest marital indiscretions, tales of opera first nights, unfortunate wardrobe choices – all of it worthy of note for the time when she would sit at her desk and describe the fatuousness of people's lives in books those same people would devour, presuming the stories to be about other people. Her work was serialised in the newspapers, one of whose writers had turned up for that evening's spectacle. Would *Tout Paris* have a scoop tomorrow morning? *We shall see*, George thought confidently.

All heads turned when the special guest arrived with his fellow pianist and friend Ferdinand Hiller. Even from a distance, George felt a tug at her heart at first sight of the delicate figure, wondering how he would survive anyone's embrace: painfully thin, with a sunken chest. He had been ill a few months before, she was told; too weak to walk, spitting up blood. Doctors had prescribed ice swallowed whole to staunch the bleeding. He had recovered to a degree, but the spectre of death looked as if it had only retreated to a back room of his apartment. Frédéric still referred to himself as a 'cadaver' when he was in one of his black moods. Such melancholy was not a good state to be in for a man of twenty-six, six years George's junior.

Like her friend Marie, George preferred the company and

the touch of younger men. She also liked tending to the injured, the broken birds of the world; to examine them, nurture them, caress them back to health. Chopin made a perfect candidate for her special brand of care, and he looked fabulous in a very elegant way on this occasion with his black fitted frockcoat and trousers, white gloves, handmade varnished shoes on his tiny feet, and the sublime touch of a white cravat knotted in one of seventy-two possible ways. He was every inch an aristocrat in monochrome.

George Sand was even more striking, dressed like a man to match her nom de plume in a frockcoat, vest and trousers, her brown hair parted in the middle and curling untrammelled down to her shoulders, a cigarette or cigar always between her fingers. Strangers pointed at her in the street. She loved the effect, the confusion she caused. Those fortunate enough to come close had no doubt about her gender. One of her greatest admirers called her a modern-day Venus de Milo.

The comparison with sculpture was lost on Chopin, who returned the scrutiny of this bizarre apparition. He leaned close to Hiller.

'Over there, Ferdinand. *That* is George Sand? Surely she's not a woman.'

Hiller followed Chopin's gaze.

'Oh, yes – it's a *she* all right, Frédéric. Rumour has it George could eat you for breakfast and still have room for croissants.'

'I am nobody's breakfast,' said Chopin.

The indignant tone was no surprise to Hiller. Like most of Chopin's friends, he doubted if the fragile Pole had ever been consumed. Perhaps he wasn't a meat eater. Frédéric never spoke about his dining history.

'Just as well, my friend,' he said, smirking. 'You don't want to end up in a kiss-and-tell book. At least anyone sharing a ménage with her wouldn't be in any doubt about who's wearing the pants.'

'I don't really have anything to say to literary women,' Chopin replied. He grabbed Hiller's arm. *'My God!* She's coming over. This is terribly forward.'

'Monsieur *Chopin*? But of course! *Bonsoir.'* George Sand extended her hand.

The two men bowed slightly. Hiller seized her hand and kissed it.

'You are correct, madame. My friend, Hiller,' said Chopin.

George noticed the thickness of his Polish accent. 'You know, we have really arranged this evening so that I can hear you both play,' she continued, smiling directly at the Pole.

It wasn't the most attractive smile Hiller had ever seen. Still, she did have an intriguing lower lip, full and slightly pendulous. A lot of sauce had dripped from that lip.

'Play, madame? I thought we were here for the conversation,' said Chopin.

'In that case, perhaps we may converse?'

'Under the circumstances, I think I should prefer to play. You will excuse me.'

He turned and walked away. George looked bemused.

Ouch, thought Hiller. *George is the perfect gentleman, and Fred's being a bitch.*

Eventually the music started from three of the greatest party pianists in Europe. Liszt and Hiller gave typically dazzling accounts, Liszt eliciting whoops of admiration from the guests during his recital after some quicksilver arpeggios. His mistress looked at him through adoring eyes; Marie knew how randy Franz became after two bottles of the best and a couple of trips around the ivories. She hoped that George would be similarly occupied enough after the end of the evening not to overhear them upstairs.

There was a break for more digestifs before Chopin's turn at the keys.

Hearing Frédéric Chopin perform was a rare event, Paris had learned. His public appearances were few. It was said that he was overawed, even frightened, of large audiences, his piano sound so soft that his artistry was almost inaudible in big concert rooms. Indeed, as his *Nocturne in D flat* floated gently through the salon George wondered how such filigree music would make it across the edge of a concert platform. The wider world was too coarse for such a quiet exhalation.

His hands were small, but the tapered fingers easily stretched across the keys; the right hand singing a sinuous melody over the rippling of the left, a song on a dark lagoon. Around the keyboard, a circle of people – their faces barely illuminated by lamplight – were drawn into the night of an interior world.

The music stopped, as did every heart in the room except George's, beating hard.

His eyes met hers briefly, then turned away. She wondered if his expression was warmer now than at their introduction; if she had fallen into his mind while his music filled the air. *He must be a supremely sensitive being*, she thought. *Could he not be aware of the feelings flowing back to him?*

'Mazurka in A minor, published as Opus 17, number four,'

Chopin said in an undertone. Most did not hear him. Again, he played.

George expected something lively and folksy; all those exuberant Polish aristocrats jumping about in their ballrooms. This music was homesick, halting, drained of energy; a melody too tired to dance. Someone alone, making futile steps in an empty space.

George felt the composer's oppressed solitude. If only she could have rushed over to him and lifted that emaciated figure from the stool. But he was sealed off from the room while he played. All she could do was look at him through the strands of smoke from her cigar and try to suppress her sudden desire for sex.

The music ended a second time, its silence merging with that of the room. Mere applause felt vulgar after such rarefied sound. Chopin glanced at George once more, and in that split second she tried to channel something to him with her eyes that would have taken days to write – even at her prodigious speed.

Then he slipped on his gloves, clutched his bespoke hat, muttered his excuses to Liszt and Countess d'Agoult, and was gone.

People whispered to each other. George saw the *Tout Paris* feuilletonist was scribbling furiously.

'What do you think he's writing?' said Madame d'Agoult, sidling next to George.

'Heaven knows. Perhaps he saw something I didn't. I know this is unlikely, but for once that idiot may have a better imagination than mine.' George felt her familiar surge of appetite. She wanted to be satisfied by someone. Tonight, the pianist was unavailable.

She noticed the so-so Swiss writer Didier casting her imploring looks from his position at the far wall. They had enjoyed a few liaisons of late when the mood took her. He was attractive – and reliable.

'Excuse me, Marie,' she said abruptly. 'We can't have fiction being spread around town.' She stubbed out her cigar and strode across the room.

'Madame Sand,' Didier said with relief. 'I was hoping we might speak —'

'Come now, Charles,' she interrupted, taking his hand. 'I want you to see me to my room.'

In the street outside, Chopin lifted the collar of his greatcoat and coughed as he and Hiller made their way back to the composer's apartment on the Chaussée d'Antin, a couple of blocks away. It was colder than usual for an autumn night.

'Madame Sand – what did you think, Fred?' said Ferdinand. George's looks at Chopin had not gone unnoticed around the salon. She had gone far beyond flirtation. She *wanted* him.

'Repulsive,' said Frédéric.

~

'You had quite a night,' said Marie d'Agoult early the following afternoon.

'I *didn't* actually,' said George, dark circles under her eyes, far from completing her toilette, already nursing her first cigarette of the day. 'Charles must have been overawed by the occasion, or my sudden renewal of interest, or something. He was very slow to get going. I had to keep at him for hours.'

'Perhaps he sensed you were thinking of someone else.'

'That's not like a man. Normally, the machinery is always willing. The *head* is of no consequence.'

There was a pause as George stared out the window, idly pinching flecks of tobacco from the tip of her tongue.

She swivelled back to Marie and said abruptly, 'There is something so noble, so *aristocratic* about Chopin, isn't there?'

'Franz says he's a genius – a complete original,' said Marie. 'I must say, I agree. His music comes from a mysterious place. Where do you think it comes from?'

'Poland, I suppose,' said George. 'I want to see him again.'

'That may be a problem. Franz told me Monsieur Chopin was not greatly taken with you.'

'He'll come around,' said George. 'All the others do.'

Two weeks later, the invitation arrived from the Chaussée d'Antin for Franz, Marie and George to come to Chopin's for dinner. Just the four of them.

Marie put down the letter and looked at George.

'You've suddenly leapt into Frédéric's inner circle,' she said. 'Was there something I missed? Something you said?'

'You missed nothing, and I said nothing,' said George. 'Our little one is just as intuitive as I suspected. He knows I will have been thinking about him.'

Marie smiled. *Really, she and Franz share an insolent confidence*, she thought. *I wonder sometimes why they didn't get together.* Some said they had, but that was typical of Paris.

Chopin's dinner was the opposite of the frivolous soirée Liszt and Marie had hosted two weeks before. Much as she would have loved to hear Frédéric play again, George felt it would have offended him to be asked. She and Liszt smoked their cigars and threw back cognac; Chopin ate sparingly, coughed a little when the fug of tobacco in the room became too dense, and drank milk.

The conversation dispensed with gossip and stuck to fact. Marie revealed a deep knowledge of politics, Liszt reminisced to Chopin about meeting George, and to George about meeting Chopin. He put down his cigar and his glass to expound on the benefits of asceticism, asserting that Art was the way to God.

'I've often thought about becoming a priest,' he said. 'God sees me and I fear that I could offend him in his presence if I don't aspire to meekness and a refutation of earthly love. We have so little time to get it right in this life. I like the words of Thomas à Kempis: "Love to be unknown, and accounted as nought".'

The others looked at him with disbelief. *Liszt*, with his smoking and drinking, his crazy hours, his music full of acrobatics. An *ascetic*?

'I don't doubt your sincerity on this, Franzi,' said Marie, 'but I wish you'd told me sooner.' She winked at him.

George raised an eyebrow, took a long draw on her cigar and glanced at Chopin.

'Don't worry, Frédéric,' she said. 'Franzi is just preaching his personal gospel for today. Like all gospels, it is frequently ignored by those who are most ardent. By his own standards, Franz is a heretic. It may be that God alone deserves to be loved, but when one has loved a man, or a woman, it is very different to loving God. And I know which I prefer,' she added, blinking slowly at Marie.

'And that would be?' Marie asked. It was a tease.

'There is only one happiness in life, Marie. To love and be loved. Franz is right about having no time to waste. *This* is our goal.'

'Madame, for women this is a recipe for captivity!' said Chopin with mock dismay. *And for men too*, he thought.

'Are we talking about love, or marriage?' asked Liszt. 'If the latter, I agree completely.'

'Not if one refuses it – or can escape from it, as I have done,' said George. 'My profession is to be free. I am now divorced, after much trouble. I don't want to represent conventional womanliness in the way I dress. I am not subject to the control of public opinion. I choose to live outside the world's prejudices; false, outdated and dull as they are. Nonetheless, I aspire to the happiness I have described. Believe me, this is no vague dream.'

She looked at Frédéric with the same intensity as at their first meeting. He was suddenly aware of her hand on his leg under the table.

'Heaven is all around us, anyway,' said Marie. 'So is Hell, in all the puerile gossip Franz and I have endured these past few years. I agree with Heine. He said that when dear God gets bored with Heaven, he opens the window and contemplates the boulevards of Paris.'

'In that case, you and I should follow God to the heavenly boulevards now, my dear mistress, and leave our friends to discuss the possibilities of finding happiness on earth,' said Liszt. 'We are going. I want to create more cigar smoke, and I fear it might not be agreeable to Frédéric's constitution. You'll be staying, George?'

'I believe so,' said George. 'The main course was splendid. I am hoping for a typically Polish dessert.' She slid her hand up Chopin's thigh.

The host's white face turned crimson, his mouth falling open.

'Madame Sand, I do not think —'

'*Please*, monsieur – call me Aurore,' she said.

'Madame . . . I have lessons to give tomorrow morning. I . . . I am very tired. Your company has enchanted me; I will spend my time in bed tonight thinking a great deal.'

'You are much too creative,' said George, without sarcasm. 'I only *think* in bed when the sun is up and I need to write. As it is,' she said, looking out the window and then at her man's pocket watch, 'we do not need to think for another seven hours.'

He looked at her, aghast. She withdrew her straying hand, deciding to end his discomfort.

'Let's go home then,' she said to Franz and Marie. 'It's late, and our friend clearly has work to do. Thank you, monsieur, for the *hospitality*.'

George looked once more at his beautiful face with its conflicted expression before closing the apartment door. *The dear, dear child*, she thought. *Is it possible that a man of twenty-six could be so charmingly innocent?*

She asked Liszt and Marie the same question on the way back to the rue Laffitte.

'Many of the young ladies of Paris wish that he wasn't,' replied Liszt. 'God knows, they're lining up down the boulevards to have lessons with him. He could probably teach them all if he didn't put aside time every morning to compose. *Some* of them must be in love with him, I suppose. Don't be fooled by tonight, George.

He's certainly not immune. In a single evening he'll convince three women at a party that he loves them all, and the next day will say nothing about it. I can't tell whether he's saving himself for someone special, or just isn't interested in that sort of thing.'

Or is simply a prude, he thought. He had used Fred's apartment for an afternoon the previous year to have a quickie with a married woman while Marie was laid up at home having their daughter Blandine, and Fred had been very snitty about it.

'Either way, George, you should consider that you may be attempting to seduce a virgin,' said Marie. 'Sometimes I look at poor Frédéric and wonder if it's a *mother* he really needs, rather than a lover.'

'I've been down that path before,' said George. Younger than she, sick, in need of nurturing back to health: she found these to be irresistible qualities in her men. She had been their mother – and with the virgins, even their teacher. How many virgins had there been? Certainly, thin little Jules Sandeau, who was curly-haired and just nineteen when she took him to the special pavilion on her estate at Nohant and watched his hormones push the colour into his cheeks while she undressed and lowered herself onto his lap. That had gone on and off for years with their leaving for Paris to live and write together, leaving her husband and his wine cellar back in the country home. She had quickly outpaced and eclipsed Jules in the world of letters, consoling herself by the end with the knowledge she had transformed him from provincial hick into a city professional. In return, he gave her a convenient nom de plume when she was ready to publish her first sole-authored novel, *Indiana*, under cover of a man's name: 'Sand', a contraction of his own.

A deflowering was just dandy, as far as the former Aurore Dupin was concerned.

Chopin lay in his bed, deep in thought. He had offered this as an excuse, and it had turned out to be a prediction. His lungs hurt from the smoke he had inhaled throughout dinner.

How wrong he had been about George Sand! He had thought her vulgar and unwomanly. Tonight, he discovered an original, eloquent thinker. There was an overpowering aura about her, a musky sense of womanhood bursting through the mannish clothes. It might have been what the writers called 'sensuality'; he couldn't be sure.

She was *magnificent*. And if she had stayed? What then? He knew, of course. But it was too much to contemplate.

He would put those distasteful visions to one side and consider instead how and when he could see her again – in the safety of company.

Or else he would work on the idea for a scherzo that had burst from his fingers while he was improvising the previous morning. Yes, the distraction of people would always take second place while he was able to work – however long that turned out to be.

There was also the matter of little Maria, back in Dresden. He could not bear the thought of Parisian tittle-tattle finding its way back to her mother, Countess Wodzinska.

If only George hadn't put her hand on his leg.

13 December

George knew she had made a supreme impression on Chopin the moment she swept into his salon for the party wearing white pantaloons and a blouse with a red sash.

Chopin's friend Count Grzymala leaned down to the composer at the piano and said, 'Your admirer has arrived, Fryderyk. My God – she's dressed like the Polish flag.'

Liszt had never seen his housemate look more beautiful: her hair glossy, the skin around her décolletage glowing bronze.

'I'll say this for George,' he whispered to Marie, 'when she presents as a woman, it's very impressive. She's the most beautiful man in the room.'

The hubbub resumed with loud conversation in Polish among Chopin's circle of Paris-based compatriots, together with the pop of champagne corks and clink of glasses. George strode over to some of the men on a corner sofa, reaching into her pocket.

'Gentlemen, who would like a *poetic* cigar?' she offered.

'What makes a cigar poetic, *mon frère?*' said the tenor Nourrit, putting one to his lips.

'More than a touch of opium,' said George, lighting it. 'You'll be spouting verse within minutes.'

'What about me *singing* some verse, with a little musical help from Schubert? Franz! Move Fred off that piano stool. Let's do a couple of songs. Friends! Listen to these *lieder* from Vienna. The poor bastard who wrote these died nearly ten years ago, barely in his thirties. Tragic. The good die young, eh?'

'I hope not,' said Chopin. 'Being bad is not my style.'

'That is the most perceptive thing I've heard you say about yourself, Frédéric,' said George from across the room. She drew hard from her cigar and fixed him with her eyes.

Sombre eyes, singular eyes, he thought. *What are they saying tonight?* His heart was captured, just for now. Would it be opened by the captor?

Nourrit sang, and then Chopin joined Liszt to play a four-hand sonata.

Grzymala walked across to George and introduced himself. He gestured to the two white apparitions at the keyboard.

'The two greatest pianists of the age, and we are able to hear them at play. It is a privilege, is it not – madame, or monsieur?' he said, with a grin.

'Either, monsieur,' she said. 'The mind has no sex.'

Liszt embroidered his *primo* part at the top end of the piano with glittering roulades, throwing musical fireworks into the air above their heads. Chopin gave his friend an admonishing smile; this sort of display was not his way, but Franz was a phenomenon.

George noticed the expression, sensing a rare moment of transparency in a person who remained a mystery to her despite the range of feelings he appeared able to express – all except one.

This was Chopin's happiness: the small room, the intimate circle of friends, the discourse of music, the bittersweet tang of transience. It explained him; it explained his music, full of regret for whatever might happen.

'Have some ice-cream, George,' said Marie, motioning to a table. 'It will cool your throat after the heat of your cigar.'

George's eyes were reddening as the cigar's poetry made its effect.

'I will savour the heat for now, Marie,' she said. 'And do me a favour: don't offer any to Frédéric. He's cool enough.'

Liszt stood up at the piano at the end of the duet, cigar propped between his lips, and reached for his coupe of champagne.

'Gentlemen, ladies, and *lady-gentleman*,' he announced, glancing at George. 'Let's drink to us all, philosophers every one of us – coming from doubt, journeying towards truth.'

'That's his second poetic cigar,' Marie said to George.

Chopin slid back to the middle of the piano stool and launched into a polonaise. Grzymala grabbed the hand of one of his friends and attempted some awkward steps.

'I *love* these artistic parties,' Nourrit called out to the room. 'The women pass out the cigars, and the men dance with each other.'

~

This time George stayed after the last guest had departed.

Together they surveyed the disarray of the room. She walked across to Frédéric and took the face she had adored from the first between her hands, bringing it to hers.

She felt a brief tremor of resistance before he yielded with what felt to her like relief.

She reached around to his thin buttocks and pressed his groin into her while they kissed. Yes, there was something there, she noticed. *The dear child is reluctant, but he is not a eunuch.*

He had been partying in a loose shirt, the same clothing he

wore while composing. She attempted to undo several buttons, to see the air of desire fill that emaciated chest.

He drew back. 'No, Aurore – no,' he whispered.

She took his left hand and placed it on her breast.

'Frédéric,' she murmured. 'Feel me. Look at me. I am dressed in the colours of Poland. This is an appeal to your patriotism. Show me the love of your country. Come to the motherland.'

'Aurore, it is distasteful to me that you conflate patriotism with *carnal* desire.' He almost spat out the adjective.

'My child, I am not talking about desire; I am talking about love. Is it wise or useful to despise the flesh of the people one loves?'

'I do not *despise* that prospect at all.'

'Then I will change the word. "Fear", perhaps.'

'I prefer "respect". The night has been so perfect, and you look so beautiful. There is so much for me to cherish already. Certain deeds could spoil the remembrance.'

George stepped back. What a stupidity. *There must be a mistress who doesn't deserve him; maybe such a disappointment between the sheets he doesn't know how good it could be.*

At least he had mentioned *respect*.

'That's the word used by someone who invokes their morality,' she said. 'Someone who wishes not to be unfaithful. Is there another?'

Maria Wodzinska. It had been a long time, and her mother ensured it was completely chaste – but those few weeks last year in her company had been so beautiful. He hoped they would meet again next summer . . .

'Perhaps. Well – almost.'

'It sounds like a situation that needs to be resolved one way or the other.'

Frédéric was not familiar with resolve, even if he was in the middle of composing a piece; some of them took him years. Vacillation was a way of extending time. It was one way he could banish all the other signs that his own time might be running out.

'I can't resolve it as quickly as that. We need more time together. Her family are aristocrats. They need to be persuaded...'

'Oh dear, Frédéric. The *family*? Let me tell you this: the pressure of family approval and the obligations imposed by society are the things that drove me from life with two children and an *approved* husband on a country estate to the liberty of an artist's life. To me, that was a positive step. You are *already* an artist – and you want to go in the *opposite direction*?'

'Only for a few weeks next summer.' He already felt less convinced.

'Then let someone who cares for you offer an alternative. Several times a year I go back to *my* estate to take the air, feel the sun and write as much as I can. Friends come and go; my children Maurice and Solange are there. Why don't you come and stay? You can compose while I write. Any countryside worth its salt needs music like yours to mingle with birdsong. You will make Nohant live. It might do the same for you.'

Chopin tried to repress his suspicion. Surely George Sand had made it clear in all their brief discourse that she wanted more from him than merely good health? And if she was motivated more by altruism than love, not even the appearance of health was something he could give her.

Still, it was a very *therapeutic* proposal. The notion of George Sand as his nurse appealed to him. Nurses and patients had to observe a certain propriety.

But leave the city? Friends, parties and flirtations, where he could carve out time for work entirely on his terms? Compared to this, the country would feel like a prison. He was fond of most routine, excepting the routine of being a houseguest.

Frédéric was overwhelmed by George's presence. In just three meetings, she had burrowed more deeply into him than any woman he had ever known. If this was love, it felt uncomfortably like a violation. He didn't know if he could endure a more prolonged exposure to those eyes. They would seek out everything, cast a light into the most remote corners of his soul. It was better that his music did that sort of work.

'Goodnight, George, and thank you for the offer,' he said. 'I will be in touch.'

Nohant, summer 1837

The afternoon sun slanting through the shutters of the bedroom drew lines of light across the bronzed back of the woman as she straddled the figure beneath her. A large pile of handwritten manuscript lay on the bedside table, the ink still wet on the topmost page where a sentence had been broken off by more pressing concerns.

George closed her eyes, partly because some men's faces looked most unflattering when they were about to empty themselves inside her. Félicien's was decent enough in repose, but

as soon as he began puffing during his animal function, clutching her hips and pulling her down to him (as if gravity wasn't
efficient enough), he developed a twitch, almost a palsy, on the
left side of his face that had the fleeting effect of making him
look considerably older than his twenty-four years. The beard
didn't help either.

What a combination, she noted, riding him more quickly:
the guttural moaning below her, and the sound of Chopin's E
major study from the Opus 10 set filtering up from the distant
piano, one describing a complete loss of control, the other the
summit of refinement.

Love songs were so sweet, so melodious. Why, then, should
the ultimate expression of love descend into such cacophony?
Perhaps that explained Chopin's resistance to the prospect of
sex; as a musician he was less concerned about the sensations
he might feel than the noise he might make.

The playing stopped mid-bar when Félicien bellowed one
long hoarse note. George felt the blossoming of his warmth
inside her. It was just like the opera; the orchestra halting
while the singer unleashed a cadenza. *How considerate of Franz
to allow the climax of this aria its own unaccompanied moment*,
she thought. *He overheard the crescendo; he understands.* As
Félicien groaned more quietly and shuddered slightly, the
music resumed.

George slid up and off the huge sprawled figure. She reached
over to her table, opened a drawer, extracted a thin cigar and
lit it.

'Sometimes I feel I could renounce all this,' she said. 'Old
age is coming. But then you reveal that extraordinary cock

imported all the way from Mauritius and I think: there is so much to *see* in this world.'

Mallefille smiled, his face straightened now, the years acquired during his orgasm falling away. He took the cigar from her fingers for a puff.

'Aurore, you're only nine years older than I am. Are you suggesting I have so little youth left?'

'My dear child, if you keep fucking me as often as this you'll bring a premature end to us both.' She glanced at the papers next to her. 'You're making it hard enough as it is to keep the words coming on *The Master Mosaic Workers*. My publisher is expecting a completed book by July.'

He handed the cigar back to her. 'We both have things to write. But it *is* spring, and old age is further away than you think.'

'Not when I see how quickly my children are growing. I should stay here and get back to work. And *you* should get back to tutoring Maurice and Solange some more before the summer's over. After all, that is *theoretically* why you're here.'

He swung his muscular frame out of the bed and dressed. George admired his shoulders as he pulled on a shirt. Félicien had been brought to the estate to teach her children, and was doing a very good job; her headstrong fourteen-year-old son was concentrating for a change. Félicien had literary ambitions, he was attractive and didn't try to conceal his interest in her as the country around Nohant burst into life. She had just ended a fling with one of her visitors, the actor Bocage, when she realised he only wanted her to write a play for him. Franz and Marie were staying; one still night she had overheard them making love in their guestroom, Marie squealing something in German during her climax.

What else was a chatelaine to do amid this convulsive cycle of nature? George had followed the natural cycles of the earth ever since childhood, when she ran through the fields around this house. She was aware of the same forces at play inside herself. So, one night she had waited until the children were asleep, and then knocked softly on Félicien's door.

'It's a nice tune, that music. I can even remember the first few notes,' Félicien said, running a hand over his close-cropped hair.

'It's by a friend of Franzi's – and mine, Monsieur Chopin.'

'*Chopin*? Liszt has mentioned a *Zo*-pin.'

'A little joke on Chopin's accent. He's a Pole. Franz and Frédéric aren't as close as they used to be. Faded friendships are a pattern in Frédéric's life,' she said. A pale face and tender spirit flashed through her mind. *The poor darling boy.*

'Liszt sure likes playing it.'

'He admires it, and he's sentimental about it. All of those Opus 10 Etudes are dedicated to him.'

'Seems a pity Chopin's not here in person, when his music floats through the place every day.'

'I've invited him several times, and I've had Franz and Marie do the same,' said George. 'But he's never replied.'

PARIS

Chopin held the unopened letter with one hand while the other gently rubbed his chest, still sore from the exertion of the previous night's coughing. His damned grippe had plagued him through the end of winter, and with it the return of those awful dreams in which Death stood behind the doors of his apartment.

There had been a time not so long ago when such thoughts were obliterated by the memory of eyes locked onto his in a room full of flowers, the warmth of a breast under his hand.

With those thoughts came guilt about Maria. The Chopin and Wodzinski families were friends from Poland; he had known Maria ever since she was a child. She had grown into a striking, articulate teenager who called him 'Frycek'. When her family relocated to Geneva and then Dresden after the fall of Warsaw, he visited them from Paris. Maria adored him; everyone could see it, and her mother encouraged it. 'Make sure you wear your long socks to bed, Frycek!' she wrote to him when she heard of his illnesses during the many months that had gone by since his last visit.

He was engaged to her in everything but name, as far as he was concerned. Not enough to *ask*, but enough to believe. George Sand was out of the way, and he would see Maria in Dresden again that summer. It had been some time since any news from her, he realised. Now those anxieties of absence were gone; Maria's handwriting was on this envelope. It had changed from her childish scrawl into the assured style of an eighteen-year-old. A woman who knew her own mind.

Chopin opened the envelope and read the letter.

The message was brief. There was no mention of a future meeting. It ended with the words: *'Adieu! Remember us!'*

Frédéric looked at the single page for a long time.

Then he collected all of Maria's other letters over the years, plus those of her mother, who used to remind him about staying warm.

He found a large envelope, carefully placed the wad of correspondence into it with the dried remnant of a rose Maria had once given him, and tied it closed with a blue ribbon.

He seized his composing pen, and wrote two words on the front of the envelope before placing it in a drawer.

My Grief!

He dabbed at his eyes with a handkerchief. There were no tears. He noticed, however, that the linen was flecked with blood.

It was back.

There was so little time left for him to be happy.

PARIS, 25 APRIL 1838

Chopin's new second scherzo filled the opulent salon in the Spanish consul's apartment, and once again George Sand stared into the face she had not seen for well over a year.

Its sensitivity struck her as much as ever, even though Chopin looked to have aged more than one would expect in that time. *Illness*, she thought. *He looks so exhausted, the dear child.*

The music itself gave no sign. This new piece glowed with a greater sense of affirmation than anything else of his she had heard, leaping out of its minor tonality as soon as it could to sing passionately in the major, its second theme arcing upwards over and over, reaching for life, grasping at fulfilment.

Something inside Frédéric had changed. Was he preparing to open himself to the world, to become more receptive to the feelings of others?

To care for him, protect him, help him to flourish – the urges she had felt from the start, stronger than that of mere physical possession, all burned through her mind. Was this, finally, a true sort of love? She thought of her isolated childhood, a silly marriage devoid of feeling, the passing gratifications from the string of lovers, and suspected that even with her knowledge of human nature and sympathy for the independent spirit, she couldn't tell if this new impulse to lose herself in that face was the 'love' that existed in the classics.

Mallefille was still down in Nohant, teaching the children by day and obliging their mother by night whenever she happened to be around. He was an excellent being, George knew: stable, virile, owner of a level temperament, sturdy as an oak; everything Frédéric was not. Almost as strong as *she* was. What could she possibly give to such a self-sufficient life force? Nothing more; and merely *receiving* him in every sense was not an option. It certainly wasn't Love.

Her turmoil must have been obvious. When she recalled herself to the present moment she noticed the music had stopped. Chopin was looking at her with a tender curiosity, silently mouthing something while the others around the piano applauded. She narrowed her eyes to read his lips.

Where have you been?

George hurried over to Grzymala. They had kept in touch

with the occasional exchange of letters during the past year.

'Wojciech, we must talk,' she said, drawing him aside as the consul's wife, Madame Marliani, led Chopin in the opposite direction to meet a blushing circle of young women.

'Madame Sand, I would prefer talk to the sterile business of writing letters,' he said, smiling. 'And we are speaking now about ... ?'

'Frédéric, of course. He looks happier, tonight, doesn't he?'

'He does, madame. And I can imagine why.'

'So can I, sadly. The last time he and I spoke, he told me about a likely engagement. Is this person going to make him happy?'

'My dear George, that's not the question you should ask —'

'I'll put it differently, if only to assure you that my concern isn't the bad fruit of some petty jealousy. Chopin's happiness, his life, are more important to me than his love. He is too fragile to resist great pain. Loving may be too much for him. If he can find restfulness with someone else, that sentiment alone may be enough. I don't want to steal anybody from *anybody*.' His face came back into her mind, the soft question he had just asked her.

Grzymala was smiling.

'This sounds terribly selfless, George. Could it be that — ?'

She cut him off again. 'At the same time, I don't want him to sacrifice himself to marriage out of a sense of duty to some childhood friend. The past is a limited thing.' She turned her gaze away from Grzymala to the small, immaculately dressed figure across the room. 'The future is infinity, an unknown. *That* is where feeling must flow.'

Grzymala was struck by the change in her face. Normally, her features were languid, almost expressionless, apart from those huge eyes. Not tonight; she was radiant with animation. The cross-dressing man-slayer that Aurore Dupin presented to the literati had it bad – and all because of his sickly, brilliant compatriot.

'George, perhaps it is equally pertinent to enquire whether *you* are being taken care of? Rumour has it so. At least, that's what a little Hungarian bird has told me.'

'There is wax at home upon which I sometimes place my seal. Someday I may wish to change the seal, and when the time comes I'll do so with patience.'

She would clear the way for Chopin, in other words, Grzymala understood.

'I'll tell this to our friend, with your permission, George,' he said. 'Because what I have been *trying* to tell you is that Frédéric is no longer engaged. He never was, in fact. And the young lady who *may* have been in question has long since been redirected towards more robust quarry by her family.'

Her mouth dropped slightly. The thin cigar halted its journey to that thick lower lip.

'Now, I'm not sure about the "seal", as you call it, but you might want to go and check on the wax.'

She felt the stare of blue-grey eyes.

~

Chopin seemed unsure of what to do, so George guided him all the way.

'Am I there?' he asked.

'You are, my dear child. Let yourself be. Move a little, if you like.'

He did so with difficulty, panting with breathlessness rather than desire. Her own feeling was less the surge of physical pleasure she enjoyed with Mallefille, more a ripple of simple tenderness. Sex would not be a large part of whatever was to come, she predicted. That was all right; she'd had her fill.

He panted harder.

'That's good, Frédéric. Let it happen.'

He stopped. The beautiful face wide-eyed in the darkness.

'Aurore, I don't know if I should void myself in this way. This is all the strength I have. If we know that feeling is there, maybe I should reserve what is left for my work.'

She ran her hands over his bare shoulders.

'Little one, it's my experience that the reservoir soon refills with creative energy. I can wake in the morning after a night like this and spend the whole day putting thousands of words onto paper. But if you're more comfortable thinking that your tea-spoon of semen will metabolise into a mazurka if left unspilled, I say: whatever keeps the music coming. Is it a mazurka tonight, or me?'

'Give me some help again,' he said, smiling.

Minutes later, Chopin reached for his handkerchief, grateful that the gloom concealed the traces of red among his spittle.

Her voice was suddenly low and musical.

'One adores you, Frédéric. Did you enjoy yourself?' she said.

He stopped dabbing at his mouth.

'Yes, George. It has been a long time.'

'How long, if I may ask?' She would need to talk to Mallefille when she returned to Nohant.

'A lifetime, I suppose.' He shook as he coughed. She sat up.

'Do you know what, my dear? We are going to make you well. You need a thorough diagnosis of what is wrong with you, a young man of twenty-eight with a rich life ahead. And I know what the doctor will recommend.'

'Sucking ice, like before.'

'No – a change of climate. I can't believe that a lifetime in the cold of Poland and Paris is good for the system. I've tried to bring you to my house in the country, and so far, you've resisted. Let's look for a solution further afield, then; somewhere in the deeper south, beyond France, closer to the warm air of Africa. My son Maurice is suffering from rheumatism, and I want him to avoid a harsh winter as well. We can all go away, escape, breathe life-giving air, feel sun on our skin. Our friend the Spanish consul tells me how beautiful it is on the island of Majorca. If you still want to be with me in a few months' time, would you come for an adventure? We'll take a piano, of course.'

Her eyes shone.

'Madame George Sand, I have to say that as of tonight, I have been thoroughly seduced,' he said, aware that Paris would soon know. What would it think?

'Is that a yes, Monsieur Chopin? If I may quote you, will you *be in touch?*'

He frowned, and sounded more serious than she expected. 'I will have to think about it for a while, George.'

'You do that, my dear,' she said, patting his thin arm before rolling over quickly to the drawer of her bedside table. 'Right now, this girl would kill for a cigarette.'

POSTSCRIPT

Chopin's and Sand's sojourn to Majorca in 1838–39 was a disaster that almost killed him. The winter was the most severe in living memory, bringing the composer's health and mental wellbeing to the point of collapse. The couple beat a precipitate retreat from both the austere and poorly heated former monastery they had rented, and the hostility of the locals who were scandalised by the unmarried visitors openly living together. Sand later documented the experience in her book *A Winter in Majorca*.

Fryderyk and George broke up in 1847 when he sided with her daughter during a long and acrimonious family dispute. They met for the last time in March 1848.

Chopin died from tuberculosis the following year, aged thirty-nine.

Bustle with the Bäsle

The world's greatest ever musical prodigy, Wolfgang
Amadeus Mozart, had his virginity maintained in early
adulthood by the constant presence of his parents.
Despite the temptations of foreign cities, the answer
to who would be the first to take the young genius to
bed was all in the family.

~

*'We do indeed exactly suit each other, for she too is inclined to be a
little wicked.'*

Wolfgang Mozart (1756–1791) in a letter
to his father, Leopold, October 1777

AUGSBURG, 11 OCTOBER 1777

'Wolfgang – you're pulling that strange face again. Try to relax
a little, dear. We'll be there soon.'

He *did* look peculiar, twisting his mouth into a rictus, one hand playing with his malformed left ear, the other drumming on his right leg. What had seemed eccentric in a child was now more than a little embarrassing for an adult in mixed company.

Anna Maria Mozart sighed. She knew what was going on inside that extraordinary head. His eyes had that glazed look. *What a pity.* The autumn colours in the countryside outside Augsburg were so beautiful; copper and yellow leaves starting to flutter down from the trees. And sitting in the coach with her was her only living son, whom any casual observer would have taken for an imbecile.

'*Wolfgang!*' she repeated. His lips snapped back together, the weak chin receded to its usual position, and the slightly protruding eyes regained their focus.

'I'm fine, Mamma,' he said, smoothing his profuse fair hair with both hands.

Mozart's mind was working so quickly, and he was so stimulated by what it was doing, that he found it impossible to control himself, channelling the nervous energy to his extremities. The *clip-clop* of the horses' feet had suggested a rhythm to him, then a tune over the top, and then another, the harmonies and the entire structure of a piano sonata movement assembling in his head without any effort. Within moments, the piece existed from beginning to end, all its internal parts completely worked out, so that he could turn it around and upside down, examine it from every angle. He put it to one side when another melody drifted in, an entirely new one, this one with the sound of a soprano's voice. An arietta was taking shape.

That made two pieces. It had been a busy five minutes.

The trick was to find a clear half-hour in which to write it all down. Wolfgang could wait, though. The finished music was filed away in his memory and would stay there unchanged until he found a stable surface and a sheet of manuscript paper. The transfer to pen and ink was a mechanical process, requiring neither peace and quiet nor any further creative thought. He could do it later while he talked to the little cousin he'd heard so much about. His *Bäsle*.

'How long are we staying in Augsburg, Mamma?' he said, addressing his mother with the same inflection as when he was five; the pitch of the young man lower, of course – but not much.

'Long enough for me to rest from this part of the journey, dear,' she said. 'Your uncle Franz has arranged a few meetings with good people in town. You can play for them, make some new contacts. And you should spend time with your cousin. She's nineteen now; you haven't seen each other since you were little. We should all enjoy ourselves before moving on to Mannheim.'

Mannheim. That was their *real* destination. Anna and Leopold both knew their son was too brilliant for Salzburg. Wolfgang had been bored by the drudgery of working for the ghastly Archbishop Colloredo, having to grind out church music to order, being treated like a servant. He had quit that summer, and the bastard cleric had responded by sacking Leopold from his duties as court musician as well.

'God will drop a turd on his head, Papa,' Wolfgang said. 'He can lick my arse. I fart at him whenever I see him. It's great to think of the smells collecting in that ermine of his. When he enters a room, everyone will know they're in the presence of a huge stinking pile of shit.' The family exploded into laughter.

Anna smiled at the recollection. *Really, there's nothing funnier than a Salzburg joke.*

'You'll need a job, boy,' said Leopold, when they finished wiping their eyes. 'Mannheim's the place, that famous court whose rays are like those of the sun, illuminating all of Germany. And when you're settled there, we'll all join you – *when* we can afford it. Meanwhile, take your mother.'

'*Papa!* I'm all grown up! I can do this alone.'

'You need looking after, Wolfgang. And to be frank, I don't trust you to behave yourself. You can stop in to see my younger brother in Augsburg on the way. He's lost all his five daughters excepting Maria Anna, and could do with the company.'

He turned to his wife. 'This trip will take at least a year. I'll miss you, my dear. You must make sure Wolfgang works hard and plays little – apart from his music, of course.'

She looked at him with moistening eyes. 'And *you* must keep well while we're away, my love. Shove your arse in your mouth and shit in the bed until it bursts.'

'Darling wife, you say the *sweetest* things.' They held each other, chuckling.

～

The carriage took them through the centre of Augsburg, past the cathedral of St Mary and rows of medieval guild houses, before turning into the Frauentorstrasse and coming to a halt before a four-storey terracotta-coloured façade.

'I wish your father was with us, my dear,' said Anna Maria. 'He was born in this house.'

She stepped gingerly from the compartment, feeling the

twinges of her fifty-six years. Wolfgang bounded out behind her, a little chevalier with his elaborate hat, vivid red coat with gold braid, and sword. The weapon rattled against his short legs as he surged past his mother to the front door now opening to the street.

'Little Wolfgang!' said Uncle Franz. 'How you've ... grown!' He faltered on the platitude because his nephew didn't appear to have grown much at all. Franz Mozart was Leopold's junior by some eight years and looked even more so because he smiled often. His older brother's default expression was a frown.

The day had clouded over. In the gloom of the front room, Wolfgang was at first unaware of the small figure by the hearth until it stepped forward to be presented by Franz.

'This is your cousin, Wolfgang: Marianne.'

Mozart's mother looked from one to the other with approval. 'Franz – you can see they're related.'

Wolfgang could see it, too. Hair the same colour as his curled out from a small embroidered bonnet, and her blue eyes were just as widely spaced, giving her face an openness and candour that so many had remarked on in him. She was as petite as her cousin, with the same hint of petulance in the shape of the mouth. He liked the slope of shoulders defined by the shawl she wore, and the way its end hung teasingly from her teenage bust.

She looked him over as well, noticing that his skin was as pale as porcelain next to the colour of his coat, and his face pockmarked like so many who'd suffered the childhood pox. He looked ready for a laugh, though – as he did right away, the unnervingly large eyes lighting up at the prospect of a week with his new playmate.

'My little cousin! Hello, cuzz-wuzz! My *Bäsle*. I'm *so* pleased to meet you, I could almost drop one from my boat right here on the floor!'

Marianne laughed more than he did. 'Away you go then, Wolfy-boof!' she said. 'Be our guest. Let's hear you sing from that end!'

Anna Maria clapped her hands with delight. 'I see the Bäsle has the family sense of humour.'

Franz pasted a smile on his face. *Must be from your side of the family.*

'Show me a piano, a spinet, a violin, a block of wood – *any-thing*,' said Wolfgang, his hands flapping. 'Now that I have a new funny-bunny, this calls for a song. My arse and I can improvise a fugue. Sing me anything and I'll turn it into an opera for you on the spot.'

The two cousins ran together out of the room, shrieking.

'He *can*, you know,' his mother said to her brother-in-law. 'Turn anything into an opera, that is. It's almost frightening.'

Franz tried not to look too dubious. He'd heard that Wolfgang was 'special'. Still, he'd expected a reputed genius of twenty-one to be more eloquent.

'Whoops, there goes another one!' the prodigy yelled from the stairs. 'Not just the wind that time! Pick it up, cousin! Chuck the muck!' They yapped like puppies.

'Takes me back to when they were just toddlers,' Franz said, hoping it sounded like a compliment.

'The joy of children, isn't it?' Anna Maria replied. 'That's Wolfgang's special quality, the purity of a child. We've tried to ensure he hasn't lost it. Pure in spirit, pure in mind, pure in body. It's our guarantee of his continuing good behaviour.'

The Bäsle sat next to her cousin at the keyboard, watching him toy with the melodies of any ditties she could name, playing them forwards and backwards, turning them into mock-Italian arias, mixing them with other tunes, throwing colours around the room. She had never felt the presence of such a powerful intellect, such a supremely organisational force – not even in church.

'Wolfgang, how do you *do* that?' She knew it was an unanswerable question.

He looked at his hands. 'You mean: do *this*?' He arpeggiated up and down the keys. 'I've been doing it since I was four. You think about it for a while at the start – and then you don't. Or you think you don't. You reach a point where *it* thinks *you*. Without it, I don't exist.'

'I don't understand.'

'Neither do I. And I don't have to. *It*,' he said, trilling a note with his fingers, 'knows everything *I* don't.' He placed his hand on his heart. '*It* has been to places still unknown to me.'

'I thought you'd been all around Europe.'

'True. I've been on the road almost half my life. But I don't mean cities and countries. I mean *feelings* – experiences.'

'That's impossible for someone of your talent!' she said with the indignation of a teenager. '*Lesser* people don't feel anything at *all*.'

'Lesser' being anyone older, of course.

'I'm not saying I don't *feel*,' he said. 'Quite the opposite. It's just that my life so far and the attentions of my dear papa have ensured I haven't been *presented* with some things.'

She laughed, and then looked at him with curiosity. 'Such as?'

'What do you think?' He started to play triplets on a major triad with his left hand, added what sounded like distant birdsong with his right, and then sang halting little phrases to the words:

Geme la tortorella
Lungi dalla compagna

'Wow, cousin – you speak Italian?' Marianne said.

'Sure! And French. More than a smattering of English, too,' he said, still playing. 'This is from an opera I wrote a couple of years ago.'

'What is it saying?'

'The turtledove sighs, far from her mate.'

'It sounds a bit lonely.'

'It is. And it answers your question.'

'Umm – I'm sorry?'

'The question of what I *haven't* experienced.'

The tonality switched to the minor, the rhythm still rocking in triplets. Wistful, but not maudlin.

'*Vogli destar pietà*,' he sang, turning to face his cousin and switching to speech. 'Don't you think the turtledove sounds like it asks for our pity?'

'I've never listened to birdsong that way. I've never really listened to *anything*, come to think of it.'

'At least the bird has felt something I haven't.' He paused for effect. 'The love of a mate.'

'If you haven't felt it, how can you write about it?'

She saw the eyes flicker down to her breasts, then return her gaze again.

'The *music* knows what I don't,' he said. 'I just go along for the ride by *imagining* how it feels. D'you think I'm close to the truth, funny-bunny?'

She blushed. 'I'm sure I couldn't say.' *Was Wolfgang trembling, just a little?*

'Others do. The soprano who first sang that aria told me I'd hit the nail on the head. Strange, huh? The notes are way ahead of me. They have a mind of their own.'

She took his hand with what she hoped was a comradely gesture, parting her bee-stung lips in a smile that pierced him to the heart.

'Well, cousin – we'll just have to hope that you catch up to them very soon.'

~

Mozart lay in bed that night staring at the ceiling, his sleep broken by the pressure of his erection. The *other* part of him with a mind of its own.

He'd been fine – well, *almost* fine – until the Bäsle held his hand. Normally he could shed his excess energy through twitching fingers, jiggling legs, contortions of the mouth. Tonight, all of it went into his cock.

Wolfgang had felt these urges for years. They literally spilled out of him some nights when he dreamed about encounters during his childhood tours: jumping into the lap of the Empress Maria Theresa, feeling the warmth of that maternal, plump body through the silk of her dress; or the startled look of Marie

Antoinette when he amused the members of the court in the room by proposing marriage. The precocious antics of a public exhibit, a freak of nature – but one whose memory still recalled the proximity of bodies he couldn't touch. His father always nearby, watching.

Until now.

At home in Salzburg he could deal with it, relieving himself on the edge of the bed, complaining to his mother the next morning about another lost handkerchief. That ruse would be more difficult here. Instead, he tried to redirect his thoughts from the Bäsle to the appointment he had later that morning with one of the local Augsburg patricians, Herr Langenmantel, who had promised Franz Mozart that strings could be pulled for a concert by Wolfgang at the Bauernstube.

'Just make a good impression, nephew,' Franz said.

As the night passed, Mozart decided on the pieces he would play for the aristocrat and his friends. He would wear his medal to show his status. *That'll impress them.*

The spike under his nightshirt grew hot as he imagined coming back to the Bäsle after such a successful interview. She would be so delighted for him that she would hug him. He would kiss her back, and she would not resist when she felt the pressure of his hips against hers. That was the dream, anyway.

A familiar warm stickiness spread over his thighs. *Damn.*

~

'That's a very big medal for such a small man,' said Langenmantel. He was only a year or two older than Mozart, but his coarse features already gave a sad preview of his appearance later in life.

Mozart bristled and rubbed his fingers along his thighs.

'It is the Order of the Golden Spur, conferred upon me by the Pope, sir,' he said.

'Pray listen, friends,' Langenmantel said to the others at the table. 'Herr Mozart is a *knight*, apparently. All by courtesy of the Pope!'

There were some sniggers. 'And how did you come by such an honour?' he continued.

'I was privileged to hear the Sistine Chapel singers in a work confined to that sacred precinct by papal decree – the *Miserere* by Allegri,' Mozart said. 'It's an elaborate setting for two choirs with nine vocal lines in all. Its beauty captivated me so much that when I returned home I reproduced the whole thing on paper, entirely from memory. The next time I heard it with my score in hand, I saw I'd made only a couple of mistakes. The Pope found out, and instead of excommunicating me for such a transgression, he rewarded me. You see it now.'

The miracle of the achievement went straight over Langenmantel's head.

'It looks like it might be worth about ... what, two ducats, Feuerbach?' he said, turning to the man next to him.

'Maybe a Bavarian thaler,' said the other.

'That's not gold, is it?' said a third. 'Looks more like copper. Adolphus, why don't you borrow Herr Mozart's poorly made version and have a better copy made?'

'May I, Herr Mozart? It's a pretty thing, and I'm sure a good Augsburg goldsmith could improve on that typically vulgar Roman design. He could remove that hideous spur in the centre, for example. Lend it to me for just the afternoon? I may be able to arrange that concert for you as a reward. *That*, surely, is important to you. As for your little trinket,' he said, sliding a small box across the table towards Mozart, 'I'm sure you don't give a pinch of snuff for it.'

Mozart reddened, his hands fluttering at his sides, mouth twitching. His speech remained totally composed.

'Your spur already looks to be growing out of the top of your head, Herr Langenmantel,' he said. 'I have one growing elsewhere that is *far* more spectacular, and I should be sorry to exchange mine for yours.' Mozart slid the box back. 'Perhaps you should take a pinch of snuff on that.'

Feuerbach half-stood from his chair, placing his hands on the table.

'Now, see here – *musician*,' he said. 'We like to think we are hospitable to visitors —'

Mozart cut him off. 'And so you have been, gentlemen.' He stood up, straightened his waistcoat and reached for his hat and sword. 'I must leave now. Might we meet tomorrow?'

Langenmantel sniffed loudly and looked away. 'I don't think I'll be here.'

'The loss is not mine. You are a set of complete bores. I wish you a good morning.'

Mozart spun on his petite feet and left.

'Wolfy-boof, you *didn't*!' Marianne said when he told her about the meeting. Her mouth fell open with shock at his audacity, even as tears of laughter streamed down her face.

'I did, and I did, and I *did*.' He intoned the repetition like plainchant, dashing to the keyboard for accompaniment. 'I did and I did. Funny-bunny, these people aren't worthy enough to eat my shit. It's a strange world where people of talent have to kowtow to dullards with money and power. One day it's going to change.'

'You may starve in the meantime, cousin.' She walked over and stood behind him at the piano stool, placing her hands on his shoulders. 'Isn't that what this whole trip is about? Another big city, another wealthy Elector, another abject request for employment?'

He flared with anger from the neck up at her words. Her *touch*, however, provoked a different reaction from the waist down. Reaching behind him, Wolfgang clasped his hands around the back of her legs, drawing her closer until he could feel her thighs against his back.

Marianne pressed her fingers further into the material of his dress coat as she felt the warmth of her own desire. The attentions of men – some of them her father's friends – had not been unnoticed of late, but she had never experienced such an instant complicity with anyone. It wasn't that blood was thicker than water, she decided; there was something about the miraculous head now cradling itself on her chest, something about the heroically independent spirit it contained, that suggested this friendship – she dared not begin to call it a *relationship* – would be a unique occurrence in her life.

Staring straight ahead, he said, 'I've written to my father about you.'

Why? she thought. 'And what did you say?'

'I said you were beautiful, sensible, kind, accomplished and gay. I *didn't* say that I would like to wash you front and back, and then go looking for your bird's nest.'

She jumped back and brought her hands to her mouth, trying to suppress an embarrassed laugh. '*Cousin!*' she gasped.

He placed his hands on the keyboard again and improvised the accompaniment to a spontaneous patter song.

'Why not? Why not? My dearest clown, *why not?* Why shouldn't we, why *shouldn't* we, I *wouldn't* know why not!' He jumped up, lifted a leg and blew a raspberry.

'Wolfgang, people will hear you!' she said, more pleased than she supposed she should be.

'No, they won't. Mamma has gone for "coffee" with Fraulein von Freysinger. That means not a drop of coffee passes her lips; two bottles of Tyrolese wine will. Unlike Papa, she knows how to have a good time.' He ran over to Marianne and quickly squeezed her breasts. 'I aspire to follow in Mamma's footsteps.'

She paused for a moment's thought before leaning forward to kiss Wolfgang on the lips, a turtledove's peck.

'You know this is all new to me,' she croaked, excitement drying her throat.

'Let's try something else to secure approval for my giving a concert,' he said, holding her waist, his erection coming on despite the jiggling of his leg. 'I'm going with Mamma to St Ulrich's tomorrow to meet the kapellmeister and the prelate, maybe play their church organ there as a demonstration. They have good connections with the city authorities.' His eyes suddenly bulged from his head, massive blue orbs. '*That's it!* You must come with me! This sweet little arse of yours will make a better impression on those august men of the cloth than *I* ever could. *Come*, won't you, little cuzz-wuzz?'

She felt his hands move around to her buttocks. 'Whatever you command, you big bed-shitter.'

~

'He's good, isn't he? Oh, he's very, *very* good.' Pater Emilian leaned against the Bäsle in the pew, his wine-tainted breath blowing warm in her ear. In the organ loft above, Mozart improvised on several tunes that had come to him that morning when he'd tried in vain to obliterate another fantasy about his cousin.

Marianne leaned away so that she could look the priest full in the face.

'I don't know enough about music to say, Father. It seems to me that he is very clever. All of Europe is in awe of Wolfgang's talent. The Mozart family is a credit to our city.'

Pater Emilian leaned in the other direction and placed his hand on Anna Maria's leg.

'You Mozarts are a credit to our city,' he said.

'We are having a difficult time trying to persuade Augsburg to celebrate the fact,' she said stiffly. 'Wolfgang has been snubbed by the patricians.'

The priest belched softly and leaned back towards the Bäsle.

'Don't you think we should try to persuade the city to celebrate this divine son of music?' he said.

Marianne allowed him to touch his knee against hers.

'We *have* tried, Father. The only response we've had so far is a fascination with Wolfgang's jewellery.'

'I say we go for coffee and work on a plan.'

'I *love* a coffee in the morning,' said Anna Maria.

In the coffee house Mozart sat to Marianne's right with his

hand on her leg under the table, Pater Emilian sat to her left with a hand on her other leg, and Anna Maria sat opposite with both hands on a goblet of Tyrolese wine.

'Herr Mozart, I will go to Count Wolfeck and Herr Stein, the local piano maker. Together, I feel sure we can persuade the authorities to present you in concert before you leave Augsburg. Unless,' he winked slowly at Marianne, 'you can find a good reason to stay?' He fondled her knee while she bit her lower lip.

'I do not presume anything, Father,' Mozart said, 'but I should like to thank those worthy people of the town who have shown us hospitality.' He fondled Marianne's other knee while she casually brushed the front of his breeches.

'Elbows on the table, Wolfgang,' said his mother.

'In that case, we should seal the deal with some music making,' said the priest, putting down his goblet.

Mozart looked at his cousin with raised eyebrows and a smirk.

'What – *here*, Father?' he said. 'I see no instruments to help us.'

'I am something of a composer myself, Herr Mozart. I wish we had the time to sit down together and discuss composition.'

'You flatter me,' Mozart said. 'If we *were* to do so, it wouldn't take long.'

'Let's sing a canon I have jotted down,' said Emilian.

'Really, Father, for all my musical skills, singing isn't one of them.'

'You'll enjoy it, Herr Mozart. It's a setting of the words "I never in my life heard anything finer".'

'Go on, cousin,' whispered Marianne. 'There could be a concert and a few florins in it.'

'I'll start, you follow,' said the priest. The tune was short and awkward. Mozart jumped in after two bars, leaning into the Bäsle and singing:

Pater Emilian! Oh, you prick. Lick me in the arse!

Emilian couldn't hear the revised text over the laughter from the patrons at other tables, for whom such an impromptu concert was a regular event at lunch. When the performance finished, the priest hoisted himself onto unsteady feet for a bow.

The Bäsle giggled and covered her mouth with one hand. The other hand she placed squarely on Mozart's erection.

22 October

The candlelight from Mozart's bedside table cast a chiaroscuro on Marianne's face.

'After such a triumph, you can't leave yet,' she said.

'It *did* go well, didn't it?' he said, his mouth grimacing and twitching, eyes flickering in the gloom. 'Best of all to have *ma trés chère niece, cousine, fille, mére, soeur et épouse* there as well.'

'Such French, Wolfy! Which one of those am I?'

'You're *all* of them.'

She stroked his hair, suddenly too timid to touch any other part of him.

'I can't decide which was best – the concerto for three pianos, or the bit at the end when you extemporised a fugue based on all the tunes we'd heard through the concert.'

'Funny-bunny, you came all the way to my room late at night to tell me this? Making no sound with your beautiful little feet on these creaky old floors . . .'

'The crowd loved you.'

He propped himself on his elbows. 'Well – now it's your turn. Say after me: *I declare myself.*'

'I – I – declare . . .'

'You indicate, you hint to me, you notify me, you let me know, you demand, you crave, you wish, you would like, you want, you *command* . . .'

'*Slower*, Wolfy-boofy!' she whispered, laughing. 'I don't have your memory.'

'Cousin, I kiss your hands, your face, your knees, and all you permit me to kiss. Say after me again: *I expose myself.*'

He took her hands. This time she felt the gathering of energy in his fingers. *It must be coursing through his whole pale body.*

The moment had arrived. Marianne took a deep breath, released his hands, and brought hers to the top button of her nightdress.

'*Expose* myself?' she said. 'Wolfgang, this is all baby talk and no action.'

He watched, fascinated, as she revealed her nakedness, then lifted the front of his nightshirt.

'I shit on your nose,' he said.

POSTSCRIPT

Mozart and his mother left Augsburg on 26 October and continued to Mannheim. They stayed four months while Wolfgang importuned the Elector for a position, without success. During this time, he fell in love with a sixteen-year-old aspiring singer called Aloysia Weber, who rejected him. Her sister Constanze would eventually become Mozart's wife.

From Mannheim, mother and son were ordered to Paris by Leopold to further Wolfgang's search for employment. While there, Anna Maria Mozart fell ill and died unexpectedly on 3 July 1778.

Maria Anna Thekla Mozart, known as Marianne, met Mozart again on only a handful of occasions, the last being in March 1781. In 1784 she gave birth to an illegitimate daughter.

The Bäsle died in 1841, outliving Mozart by fifty years. She never married.

PLEASURE IS THE LAW

Claude Debussy ushered classical music into the
twentieth century with his sensual Prelude to the
Afternoon of a Faun in 1894. An iconoclast with a rapier
tongue on those occasions when he could be bothered
to speak, he was a lover of good food, tasteful décor
and beautiful women. By 1904 he was the most
celebrated musical revolutionary in Europe, but his
reputation would be almost destroyed by scandal.
The damage to others was even more extreme.

~

*'Life has its dangerous turning points ... Try to understand me and
not be resentful.'*

Claude Debussy (1862–1918) in a letter
to his first wife, Lilly, July 1904

58 RUE CARDINET, PARIS, JUNE 1903

The two young women slept together naked, as nymphs do on a hot day. He put down his flute and swept them up, laying them on a dry bed of reeds to proceed with the seduction.

The pair woke in a flash, took fright and ran off, leaving him there half-drunk, scratching his goat flank, wondering if they'd been there at all. Picking up his instrument again, he tried to resume his tune, but it came out sounding droopy. The shimmering air around him turned day into night, his flute sounding now like women's voices floating over a sea tinted silver by the moon, singing a siren song to him, gloating over their abandonment of him to the waves, laughing as they passed into the darkness. The sea became a river, rushing off to eternity. Nature shivered, telling him to taste all the charms of the world before his youth was swept away by the churning waters.

There was music in all this, sounding very familiar.

Daylight pierced his eyes. He rubbed them and sat up, aware of clattering coming from the kitchen nearby and the crunch of wheels on the avenue de Villiers five floors below.

A young woman's head poked gingerly through the door of the study, her fair hair tied back, her pale face smiling when she saw him.

'Hello, sleepy head,' she said. 'Another late night, I see.'

'What time is it?' His voice was gruff, as always.

'Eleven,' she said.

He'd had a good eight hours of sleeping like a baby. Apart from the dreams.

'Pleasant dreams?' she asked.

'Nothing I can remember,' he said. 'There was no point in telling your wife about dreams involving naked women. But what in the hell was all *that* about? All the charms of the world, rushing away to eternity, the soundtrack of his own music: *Prelude to the Afternoon of a Faun*, the final section of his *Nocturnes*, and one of his old songs, written years ago ... what *was* it?

'Erik will be here in an hour for lunch.'

'He'll want the usual: lamb cutlets and eggs. *I'll* do them.'

'That's fine, Claude. Nobody does eggs as well as you.' The pretty head withdrew.

Debussy looked around his small study, past the upright piano in Brazilian rosewood against the far wall and the Oriental rugs on the floor, to the work desk where piano sketches of his latest project for orchestra were stacked in front of the blotters, pens and Chinese figurines he always kept so carefully placed. *La Mer* had filled his mind with childhood memories of the Normandy coast, recollections of Turner paintings, and prints of Japanese seascapes as he wrestled with the notes at two o'clock that morning, and he'd taken the teeming visions into sleep when he took a break on the chaise longue. No wonder he'd been dreaming.

Watery dreams; *sexy* too, he observed, running the yellowing fingertips of his left hand through the thick jet-black hair plastered across his large head, the fringe pushed to one side by the oddly projecting forehead; his right hand scratching the profuse goatee attached to his sideburns by a thin ridge of beard. Not actual sex, but the *possibility* of sex.

Debussy thought it an odd dream for someone who'd been married for less than four years to an ex-model with the most perfect body he would ever know. Lilly would never engage him in any meaningful discussion about music – or *anything*, for that matter – but he hadn't thought twice about dropping green-eyed Gaby after all those years together once he'd taken Lilly to bed, writhing in a frenzy while she nibbled every part of his body like fresh pastry. It was such a pity that Gaby had shot herself.

Claude hated most talk, especially small talk. Why on earth would he rush anyone off to the altar for mere conversation? He'd said to a friend's wife only the other day that artists gave themselves to Love without calculation, their eyes closed. Claude found closing his eyes difficult when Lilly took her clothes off.

Not once in those four years had Lilly shown herself to be anything other than completely devoted to him, despite their poverty. They couldn't even afford to get married back in 1899 until Debussy banked the proceeds of that morning's music lesson. Things were beginning to improve since the success of his opera *Pelléas and Mélisande*, but it was still a stretch. Lilly took it in her stride: the daily haul of shopping up five flights of stairs, the preparation of food treats to keep him going through the day, turning unwanted visitors away while he worked.

Claude knew he couldn't ask for more from his wife. He remembered the gushing prose he had lavished upon her in letters just before their marriage; all that business about wanting the 'happiness within the beauty and charm of everyday things'. Lilly delivered the everyday in spades. He'd been happy for a while, telling his friends it was 'a time of spring'.

But this spring had turned into autumn. He could feel the temperature of their relationship dropping – at least on his part;

Lilly, he was sure, had no idea. Perhaps that was to be expected from a childless marriage no longer new. It was better they didn't have to speak about serious things, or even speak all that often, because when they did the sound of her voice made his blood run cold.

'Erik! You must scold Claude for me,' Lilly said over lunch. Debussy winced.

'Very well, madame,' said Satie. He wore the same corduroy suit as in all the previous lunches *chez* Debussy. Glaring at his friend through pince-nez, he said in a falsetto, 'Claude, you are naughty. This is your mother speaking.' He looked back at Lilly. 'There – you have it. Now, why the reprimand?'

'Claude has a pupil whose mother runs one of the most fashionable salons in Paris.'

'Who is this, Claude?'

'Emma Bardac. Her son Raoul comes here for lessons.'

Satie sat forward in his chair.

'Emma *Bardac*? The wife of that rich banker? Wasn't she Fauré's ...?'

'*Friend?*' said Debussy, with a faun's grin. 'Yes indeed. Very, *very* good friend back in the '90s. It went on for years. He wrote music for her to sing, piano pieces for her daughter, Dolly. He was almost like a *father* to the girl.' He looked at Satie from the corner of his dark eyes, and the two sniggered.

'She has these wonderful musicales where *all* the important people go,' Lilly continued. 'Sometimes they play Claude's music, and she very much wants him to be there too.'

'Given her history, I'm not surprised,' said Satie. '*Pelléas and Mélisande* made adultery very fashionable in Paris. Not that it's ever really been *out* of fashion. Look at Fauré. Pushing sixty, and he still keeps a mistress in her own apartment.'

'That sort of thing costs money,' said Debussy. 'Which is why we're still together, chérie.'

He looked blankly at his wife, and they all laughed after an awkward pause.

'I'd like to think that love has something to do with it,' Lilly said.

'That it does, my dear,' her husband replied, the face once likened to that of an Assyrian prince a complete mask.

'Madame Bardac has invited Claude any number of times, and he won't go.'

'Claude, we are talking about a *banker's wife*,' said Erik. 'Why won't you go?'

Debussy shrugged the question aside with a child's reply. 'I don't know.'

I *know, old friend*, Satie thought. *You just don't like more than a handful of people at a time – and then only the ones you know.* 'Give it a try, Claude. It might be a good thing. Success in Paris is about making connections. That is why *I* have no success; I don't like to connect. Besides, Madame Bardac is reputed to be an excellent singer; Fauré composed his *La bonne chanson* for her. She might pick up some of your songs.'

Debussy remembered the last song in that cycle, set to poor dead Verlaine's poetry: *'L'hiver a cessé'*. Some affairs stripped one's branches bare; Madame Bardac had obviously put the leaves back on Gabriel Fauré's tree.

He noticed Lilly and Erik staring at him, and shrugged again.

ONE WEEK LATER

'Monsieur Debussy! This is too marvellous!' said the petite woman with curly auburn hair. Her topaz eyes twinkled at him. 'Raoul said you might be coming, but I never hoped —'

'It's nothing,' grunted Claude, bowing slightly. 'Excuse me.' He melted away to the far side of the room.

Emma Bardac collared Raoul and nodded in Debussy's direction. 'He doesn't say much, does he?'

'Only in select company,' her son replied.

'It doesn't get much more select than this,' she said drily. 'I thought you said he was poor. He looks pretty strapping to me.'

'He says he takes after his mother. Debussy is more of a *gourmet* than a gourmand. He never eats to excess, and whatever he prepares must be of the highest quality. I think that's where all the *Pelléas* receipts went: good food, and books, engravings, Oriental knick-knacks.'

Debussy found a chair near the piano and affected an air of ennui while nursing a cigarette. *Shy, clumsy at hiding the fact, fastidious in his tastes, a connoisseur in most things*, she read in his face. *I know the type: Not very tall, dark, handsome in a strange way, imperious. Completely brilliant – and married. As am I. Don't go there again, Emma.*

She had a little surprise for him, though.

'Dear guests, *mesdames et messieurs*,' she announced, standing next to the piano, 'we can't have a musicale without music! Today I would like to sing for you one of the most beautiful chansons from the creator of *Pelléas*, who honours us with his presence today.'

Surely not the reclusive *Debussy*? The gathering murmured its surprise and applauded.

When Emma launched into '*Beau soir*', Debussy sat up with a start. *That* was what he'd heard in his bizarre dream the other week. How old was he when he wrote it – nineteen, twenty? So long ago. Memories of Marie Vasnier came flooding back: the 'mature' singing student married to an inspector of buildings, the older woman who was the first to seduce him. Claude had worshipped her, writing more than twenty songs for her – including that one.

It wasn't bad, he realised. The harmonies would have appalled his Paris Conservatoire teachers – they still did – but the sense of vanishing youth, time already ebbing away, tasting 'all the charms of the world' (*that's the phrase that came back in the dream!*) as Bourget's poem said; it all felt sincere, a slightly cloying perfume from the enraptured heart of a teenager.

Emma Bardac's voice was small, but true; pitch good, no playing about with the rhythms. When she arrived at the climax, the high long F-sharp on the word 'beau', it filled the room, exhausting itself before falling back almost an octave to an undertone, the message of youth followed so quickly by death. He wondered if those around him would think that too. No matter. He didn't care either way if his music made people *think*; it was enough for him if his music made them *listen*. Only listen. If that broke the Conservatoire's rules, so be it. That was his motto: *Pleasure is the law*.

His reverie was broken by applause. Madame Bardac came over; Debussy stood to kiss her on both cheeks. Although not a great singer, she had the instincts of a true artist, her intelligence shining through.

'May I, monsieur?' She motioned to the chair next to his.

'Mmm.'

There was a pause of a minute or two.

'You say nothing, monsieur. It doesn't bother me.'

'I *could* say thank you, naturally, madame, and I would mean that most sincerely. But I find there are only two types of people. The first are those with whom one has nothing in common, usually because they are ignorant. Talking to them is pointless. The second are those with whom one might have some true commonality. In this case, they already know as much as you do, in which case talking to them is unnecessary.'

'That makes perfect sense,' she said, knowing already that he was testing her. 'You realise that obliges you to say nothing to most people.'

'It *does*, fortunately,' he said. 'You see, the trouble with *most people*, madame, is that they don't very much like things that are beautiful. Beauty is so far from their nasty little minds.'

'That being the case, you may have to make room for a third category of person. A small one, admittedly, with just enough room for me.'

'And that category would be . . . ?'

'The person who lives for beauty, reveres those who make it, and whose *little mind* would give anything to share even a small part of their knowledge.'

He smiled. 'These are the charms of the world you talk about.'

'I know. I heard about them in a song.'

'Agreed, then. For you alone, I will make a special place.'

'We can talk, then?'

'With pleasure, Madame Bardac.'

'How would you like to begin?'

'I suppose I should say *thank you*.'

When Debussy climbed the five flights of stairs to the apartment late that evening, Lilly was waiting up to ask how things had gone at the Bardac salon.

'Fine, my dear, fine. Madame Bardac even sang one of my songs. You should have been there.' *No, you shouldn't.*

'Did you and she have any chance to talk?'

'Hardly a word.'

'That's a pity, Claude. Are you going to work now? Jump back and swim in *La Mer*?' She giggled at her own joke.

He felt a sudden lust for her. The words of that old song made him nostalgic. Somewhere close was the Claude Debussy who'd praised those red lips of hers a few years before.

'We'll *all* be in that sea soon enough, Lilo. Look outside – the night is beautiful. We are both in the stream. As it goes to the sea, so we go to the grave.' *That's what* 'Beau soir' *says. Funny how the words are more banal when you take the music away.*

'That's a no, then? Would you like me to stay and talk to you?'

'It's a *no* to work, and a *no* to talk. Stay there a moment with your mouth open a little – just like that.'

He pulled her lips to his, running his hands up under her dress.

FOUR DAYS LATER

'Claude told me he loved me this morning,' Mary Garden said to Lilly.

The Scottish soprano had been a trusted friend of the Debussys since her stellar incarnation of Mélisande in the opera's premiere the year before. Lilly knew Claude doted on her.

'That should be no surprise, Mary!' Lilly said. 'We *both* love you; you know that.'

'We're not talking about that sort of love, darling. To be precise – and it's not as if I would forget such a thing – Claude said he was *obsessed with love* for me.'

'*Obsessed?* That sounds rather more serious.' Lilly looked strangely unperturbed.

'It is. It *is*.'

'What did you tell him?'

'You know what Mélisande sings at the beginning of the opera? Her first lines? *Don't touch me, don't touch me.* I told him he was in love with Mélisande, not me. I said we three were friends and this was most precious to me. And I told him I would always love him as a great musician, but not as anything else.'

Lilly breathed a sigh of relief and took Mary's hand.

'I'm *so* glad you shared this with me, Mary,' she said. 'I'm relieved you think it's Mélisande he's besotted with, and not you. And even if it *was* you, you're the only woman in the world I could bear to take Claude away. I can't *imagine* what I'd do if he left me for anybody else.' Her smile was serene.

Mary Garden looked at Lilly Debussy with a stab of pity. *My poor Lilly – where does this leave you?*

JUNE 1904

'Your letter asked that I come, Claude. Here I am.'

Emma Bardac looked around Debussy's small study for the first time. All their previous meetings during the past year had taken place at her apartment over dinners and teas, usually with her husband or the staff nearby.

She remained the sole occupant of Claude's third category of person, the one to whom he devoted as much time as he did to the surging waves of *La Mer*, now putting on its orchestral clothes. Green and gold eyes, blue sea, fluttering like bats around the steeple of his iron-grey soul.

'Where is your wife?' she said.

'Visiting her parents,' he replied. 'These days I ask her to give me some peace when my thinking meets a block.'

'Has your thinking met a block?'

'Not at all. I spend a long time collecting impressions before I write them down. Right now, I'm just – collecting.'

'It looks as if you're collecting Verlaine's poetry again. Your letter quotes him: "It rains on the town …"'

'You know the beginning? I'm using that one in some new songs I'm dedicating to you.'

'"It rains in my heart" – of course. You mention wanting to talk to me alone.' Her gaze softened. '*Why* is it raining in your heart? What is it you want to tell me that requires such privacy?'

'Nothing,' he said.

'Nothing?' She was puzzled.

'Not words, anyway,' he said. 'Increasingly, I find words are useless.'

'Sounds like we're back to where we started a year ago.'

'I would like to play for you,' he said, indicating the piano. 'Nothing in particular, nothing on paper, nothing I or anybody else has written. Just – everything that can't be said. It will be more tasteful this way.'

Tasteful? 'You will improvise, Claude?'

'Something like that. Take a seat.'

He closed the windows and drew the curtains to shut out the street clamour and the light of the afternoon. In the darkened room, his hands glowed as pale as the ivory keys.

The music was strange, buoyed by harmonies even stranger than the ones Claude ever allowed into print. She knew they would never find their way onto paper. He was making colours, applying paint to a door that, once passed through, would be closed firmly behind them both. He was making an invitation. More than that, he was seducing her. There was no doubt about it.

Emma had done this before: the meaningful stares over soup at her husband's table, the way an admirer watched her lips when she spoke one of her celebrated *bon mots*, the exquisite tension between them when they greeted each other in a room full of other people, the surreptitious brushing of hands at the table of hors d'oeuvres. The last time had been with Fauré ten years ago, and it had gone further very quickly. Claude was more cautious about doing anything overt; it was difficult to read anything in that face, those mysterious dark eyes. She had begun to wonder if it was all just a game for him. The letter that morning came as some surprise.

They were the same vintage, she and Claude: forty-two.

Mid-life was a good time to revisit all this, to see the signs more clearly. If only she'd known the half of it when she married Sigismond so long ago! Seventeen, she'd been. What did *anyone* know at that age?

Now, at least, she knew who she was and what she needed. And as accommodating as Sigismond had been – offering her a life of security and looking the other way when she had an *amour* with someone from her artistic circle – Emma realised she needed something else. The time had come to enter another door.

There would be a scandal, of course. Paris would talk about it for *days* until the affair was superseded by the next one. She wondered if Claude considered how it might affect his wife. Sigismond would be fine; he'd find solace in the consoling pats from others at his club, or the arms of expensive consorts. With Lilly, Emma wasn't so sure. Sure, she'd probably seen something of the demimonde and the appalling behaviour of men during her time as a mannequin – but there was something *fragile* about her.

Emma shook her head, straightened herself and returned to the music. This was becoming too fanciful. Wasn't she getting ahead of herself? Claude was playing the piano for her, that's all. He wasn't saying anything, and she hadn't decided anything. *Middle age, old girl. Deep breaths.*

The recital lasted an hour, during which Debussy's body stayed immobile apart from the movements of his arms. There was a long gap where the music merged into silence, the quiet becoming an essential part of the meditation, before he finally lifted his hands from the keyboard.

He turned on the stool to look at her, one eyebrow raised as if to repeat the unspoken question.

Time to decide. *Now.*

'Yes,' she said.

Lilly was incredulous when he made the proposal later that week.

'Again? This *afternoon*? Claude, I won't even have time to let them know I'm coming! What will they think when I arrive unannounced with a suitcase?'

'Your parents will be delighted by the prospect of enjoying their beloved daughter for a month without the presence of her surly husband. Paris in July, Lilo! Why would you want to spend the month sweltering all the way up here on the fifth floor?'

'What about *you*, darling?' He could tell it made no sense to her at all. She was incapable of seeing the enormity of what was going on.

'I'll go somewhere too for a spell, *ma petite*. The trouble isn't so much *La Mer*. I've got to find something new, instead of revolving in the same old circle of ideas. If I don't, my reputation will suffer, and so too will my livelihood – such as it is. We can't go backwards from here, Lilly. We've had quite enough of living like this.'

She started to cry. 'Claude, Claude – I don't understand . . .'

'I want you on the train as soon as possible, Lilly. All these explanations will make sense to you very soon. Right now, let your parents hear your laughter. It'll delight them as much as it delights me.'

Lilly lifted her face from her hands to see if the expression on his face matched the concern of his words. It was the same impassive mask.

July

Jacques Durand put down his knife and fork and leaned forward to make sure André Messager would hear his lowered voice.

'That's part of the mystery solved,' Debussy's publisher said. 'Claude's in Jersey.'

'*Jersey?*' said their mutual friend, who'd conducted the premiere of *Pelléas*. 'He goes to a resort for the summer – *without* Lilly?'

'She's terribly confused, the poor woman. He's just written to me to say his work is going well. You'd think he could put the pen down for a holiday in July, especially with someone like Lilly on hand to fan your face when it gets a bit hot. Claude's trying to make it sound like a research project. You know – if you're writing a piece about the sea, it's better to be close to the real thing. He says the sea has shown him all its guises.'

'I remember when we were rehearsing for *Pelléas*. He needed to be close to Mary Garden as well – and not just during work hours. I bet Claude wouldn't have minded seeing all *her* guises. It was almost as if he imagined himself the Pelléas to her Mélisande.'

Durand put down his wine glass. 'He's working out there in the Channel, though. I also received a small set of songs from him, all of them settings of Verlaine. He made one rather mysterious request about publication.'

'Claude always likes to keep us all guessing. What's this one?' said Messager.

'He wants the dedication to say "In gratitude for the month of June 1904 – A.l.p.M". He says it's a contribution to legend.'

The conductor considered this briefly. 'Do you think it's some sort of code?'

'It looks more like an anagram to me.'

'*A.l.p.M* – you could be right. Where was he last month?'

'Right here in Paris. It's not the anagram of a *place*, in my opinion. I think it refers to a person. And I *don't* think that person is Lilly. She doesn't even know where he is.'

Messager sighed and reached for his wine. 'Another typically Parisian situation,' he said. 'We're both able to deduce what's going on. I just hope it all ends in the usual way so the woman can return to some peace of mind. *Contribution to legend*, indeed. Claude is a genius on a good day, but then he becomes just another arrogant prick.'

58 rue Cardinet, 13 October

Debussy's father had just left. Lilly slumped in a chair and looked across the room to Claude's desk with the blotters and Chinese figurines still in their place.

So that was it, after three months of not knowing.

Sure, his letter back in August requested a separation. But Claude had been through a lot of stress while writing *La Mer*. Special people like him needed to retreat for a while, make some room for their imaginations. At least, she supposed so.

And they were *married*. She had done everything she could to make his life a comfortable one. He used to write that her love was 'Wisdom in its most beautiful form'. 'Let's never demean it,' he said. She kept all his letters.

She was prepared to wait, but she wanted to know where Claude had gone. Just to *know*. His father had told her he would find out.

Dieppe. Claude had spent time in Jersey, and now he was in Dieppe. Another place by the sea. She knew that *La Mer* was still being completed, but how much damned sea did he *need*?

'Lilly, you must be strong now,' Debussy senior had added. Claude was not alone.

He was living with that 'society' woman. That *Madame Bardac*.

'We'll try to talk some sense into him, Lilly. Leave it to me. Promise me that you'll be all right for a few days.' *He is a dear old man.*

'I promise, Papa. We have friends I can call on. I'll make some plans.'

Now that she was alone, she stood up and walked across the room to open the drawer of Claude's desk where the revolver was usually kept. It was still there.

She was amazed at her composure, her clarity of purpose, and wondered if Gaby had felt the same before she did this.

First, she sat and wrote a short letter to Claude addressed to his father. Racing downstairs, she handed it to the concierge for the next post.

She returned upstairs in slow steps, pausing to look out the window of each landing at the trees shedding their leaves. It was three o'clock.

When she reached their apartment, she closed the door, returned to the study and retrieved the gun, carefully inserting a bullet. Then, with trembling hands – Lilly had never handled a loaded weapon before – she turned the gun on herself, pointed the end of the barrel below her left breast, and pulled the trigger.

POSTSCRIPT

Lilly Debussy survived her self-inflicted gunshot wound, although the bullet remained in her body until her death in 1932.

The scandal of her suicide attempt engulfed Paris and turned Claude Debussy into a social pariah. Most of his friends, including André Messager and Mary Garden, broke their ties with him. His divorce from Lilly was finalised in August of 1905.

The financial settlement of Emma Bardac's divorce from her husband was resolved very much in his favour due to the circumstance of her adultery. She and Debussy had a daughter, Claude-Emma ('Chouchou'), in October 1905, and were married in January 1908, staying together for the rest of his life. It was to Emma that he dedicated the second set of *Fêtes galantes* songs published by Durand in September 1904; 'A.l.p.M' was the acronym of '*à la petite mienne*' ('To my dear little one'), *chère petite mienne* being Debussy's nickname for his lover.

La Mer was first performed in October 1905 and given the thumbs-down by critics as retribution for the Debussy/Bardac episode. It is now considered one of the supreme orchestral masterworks of the twentieth century.

Claude Debussy died of rectal cancer on 25 March 1918 in Paris. His daughter, Chouchou, died the following year.

It's Not You,
It's Me

He was classical music's most eligible bachelor
during the 1850s: young, beautiful, and gifted. Johannes
Brahms was in his mid-twenties and on the cusp of
success with one of the greatest piano concertos ever
written when he took a fateful holiday to an idyllic
university town. There, he would encounter love,
inspiration, and a crucial choice between two women
in his life. Most importantly, he would face his most
intractable problem: himself.

~

'How delightful to run your hands through such hair!'
Joseph Joachim to his friend Johannes Brahms (1833–1897)
about Brahms's fiancée, Agathe von Siebold

Hamburg, spring 1858

'What do you mean, you *don't want to go?*' Joachim said, waving the letter. 'Just read what Julius promises: "good voices lodged in very lovely girls". Apparently, they will "take pleasure in being at your disposal". Hello, Mister Choirmaster! You're twenty-five, buddy. It's summertime. You're a nature boy. Surely you feel a bit of *sap* rising? Here's your chance to *dispose* of some of it.'

At the word 'dispose', the violinist poked his accompanist in the crotch with his bow.

Johannes swept back his fair hair and narrowed his eyes. 'Look who's talking, you misanthrope,' he said, only partly as a joke. 'Clara's giving me hell about this as well. She wants to bring *five* of her kids, for heaven's sake.'

'That's a holiday, then! Means she's leaving two of them behind.'

Brahms fell silent, as he always did when it came to divulging intimate details – even to his best friend. Clara had done more than complain about his reluctance; she'd brought up the old issues of 'longing' and 'unspeakable woe' he thought to be long settled between them.

Joseph saw the pale-blue eyes grow distant, and broke the reverie.

'Johannes! Don't go drifting back into your piano concerto.' He and his workaholic Hamburg colleague were giving the concerto its first public run in Hanover in January, before it headed for the big time in Leipzig.

'Well, it *is* the biggest thing I've done yet,' Brahms protested, 'making its way in a centre of European music, and the first movement still refuses to be properly born. On top of that, I'm starting on a serenade.'

'You can develop your serenade by trying it out on those Göttingen lovelies, then. Johannes, some of us want to see you enjoying yourself away from manuscript paper. We've already had a run-through of your magnum opus with the Hanover orchestra and it's shaping up brilliantly. Get your nose out of that score, dammit. Rub noses with a pretty singer or three instead. And if you're worried about temptation, Clara will be there to hold your hand.'

'*Okay* – okay, Jussuf,' Brahms said, holding his hands in the air. 'If it shuts you up, and it makes her happy, I'll do it.' He looked around the apartment he shared with his parents, brother and sister. 'Come to think of it, a bit of space for a few weeks isn't a bad idea.'

Göttingen, July

'Maestro!' Julius Grimm bounded down the stairs as Brahms was shown through the front door. 'It's been such a long time! Our ladies' choir became too much of a lure, eh?'

'Not at all.' The young Turk was already notorious for his brusque manner. 'It's good to see you, Julius. Düsseldorf feels so long ago.'

'Call me Ise, like everyone does here. Soon you'll meet my wife, Pine. And here,' he said, holding up a toddler, 'is our little one, Johannes. I wonder who he's named after?'

Brahms was touched. 'My dear man!' he said, attempting to

embrace his friend, little Johannes wriggling between their two bodies. Both men laughed.

'You're comfortable in your room around the corner? There was no room at *this* inn once Clara decided to bring so many of her family.'

'Truly, Ise – I'm having a break from family.'

They both remembered only too well those sad days in 1854, when Brahms moved into the Schumann house in Düsseldorf to help Clara with her large brood after Robert was taken away to the asylum. He was a godsend at first, but the dynamic became complicated: he and Clara fell in love with each other, writing passionate letters whenever they were apart. By the time Robert died two years later, the couple had to decide on their future.

Brahms was resolute: he and Clara were each other's most trusted confidant – but that was all. These days he still had the distinct feeling Clara kept the flame of romance alive; she sometimes behaved as if she owned him. He didn't appreciate feeling like anyone's captive, worrying that this was what future domesticity might be like – living in a cage.

Julius, on the other hand, looked like he thrived on his captivity, marrying a local girl, starting a family. And as cages went, Göttingen was an attractively gilded one: the historic brick buildings in the old town, the modest size, the cobblestones and ivy, the charge of youthful energy from the students at the colleges. Grimm was director of music in this enclave, running a ninety-voice choir named the Cäcilienverein after the patron saint of music, and some smaller all-women groups. Brahms thought he looked blissfully happy.

'Some of the women are coming around tonight to rehearse,' Julius said. 'You've picked a good time to arrive.'

And you've picked a good time to rehearse, you sly dog.

'It *is* fortuitous. Ise, you're not *up* to anything, are you?'

Grimm placed the fingertips of both hands on his chest as if offended by the accusation. '*Really*, Johannes – mix a young blond gentleman destined for a brilliant career with a roomful of equally young women musicians at the beginning of a holiday? Surely you don't think me capable of anything so obvious?'

They looked at each other, heads cocked. Then they laughed again.

Late that afternoon the prattle of baby Johannes was subsumed into a sea of exuberant voices growing louder by the minute as more of the choristers arrived.

'Johannes! Get in here!' yelled Grimm. The composer stepped gingerly into the large parlour and was met with a sea of faces, most of them his own age. An older woman with wary eyes followed him.

'Ladies, I present to you two of the foremost musicians of the age: the legendary pianist Frau Clara Schumann, and a young man whom the late Robert Schumann declared the successor to Beethoven – Johannes Brahms. They're going to spend time with us this summer.'

Clara looked decidedly uncomfortable. Brahms felt for her. She was not yet forty, yet the juxtaposition of her care-worn face with the panorama of freshness in this room wasn't flattering. Life had been harsh to the person who on a good day was still one of the most beautiful women he had ever seen. The tragedy of Robert's death, the strain of raising and supporting seven children almost single-handed, the continuing tension between her and Johannes after his decision that their being a married couple was out of the question; it had all taken a toll. There was no getting around it – she was fourteen years his senior. The difference in their ages never looked more obvious than right now. None of this impacted on their closeness or took away their history, but neither was it going to exclude him from what might be in store, he decided.

Pine Grimm plucked a young woman from the gathering and led her by the hand to Brahms.

'Johannes, I want you to meet a very special friend of the family, one of our finest singers in the group. Agathe von Siebold, *this* is our child's namesake – and just as gorgeous too, don't you think?'

'Really, Gur!' said the girl with mock indignation. 'What am I to say to that?'

'Gur?' echoed Brahms, eyebrow raised.

'That's our nickname for Pine,' she said. 'In return, they call me Gathe – as you must do. We're a little trio: Gur, Ise and Gathe.'

'You know what they say about trios.'

'No, I don't. *What* do they say?'

'A trio is just a quartet that can't get along.' He smiled and looked about sixteen.

'You've just made that up, haven't you?' She smiled back.

'I have, in fact.'

'Presuming it's true, we'll just have to make up a quartet, then. Depends if we get along.' She hadn't blushed at all. Brahms liked that.

'It's like any ensemble,' he said. 'You play together and wait to discover how good the music is.'

Clara cleared her throat behind them.

Pine stepped forward. 'I'm so *rude*, Frau Schumann. Allow me to take you around the room.'

'That's a good idea, my dear,' Clara said, a trace of acid in her voice. 'I've always found that quartets exist in their own world.'

Hypnotised by the vision in front of him, Johannes was unaware of the sarcasm. He was still taking in the lushness: rich dark hair that, when loosened, would fall past her shoulders, a curvaceous figure owing nothing to the trickery of restrictive undergarments, her high, generous bust and sumptuous hips on either side of a slim waist. Joachim had described the attributes of the Grimms' 'dear friend' before Johannes set out from Hamburg, comparing her voice to an Amati violin. *Jussuf was right about the presentation*, Johannes thought. *Now to the voice and the musicality. I'll jump on the piano and we'll find out, shall we?*

'Let's hear some of your charges, Ise!' he commanded, almost sprinting to the stool, his long hair shaking down each side of his face. 'Your friend first: Fräulein Siebold.'

'*Oooo-err!*' crooned the gathering, pitch rising and falling, a playful accusation that something was already afoot. Agathe handed Brahms some music. He saw with pleasure it was a song by Schumann, 'The Walnut Tree'.

'You choose well, fräulein,' he said quietly, glancing at Clara.

Agathe stood in the bow of the piano, facing Brahms, hands clasped loosely above her abdomen. He began to play, the right-hand refrain arching up in the very first bar, starting a delicious call-and-answer with the voice.

The immediate complicity between singer and pianist was apparent to everyone; a hush fell over the room. Agathe was enraptured, looking at Johannes with astonishment while he read the notes of the rippling piano part with ease, swaying slightly with the music's lilt, closing his eyes to savour each vocal entry.

Her voice softened into the whisper described in the text, the blossoms of the tree telling a girl their prediction of marriage as she falls into sleep, Schumann's short phrases taking the voice into the low register, the whole disappearing into a dream.

When Johannes finished, he finally locked eyes with Agathe for as long as the afterglow of the music lasted. What need did he have now to ask very much about her, he thought, since she'd described herself so completely with her singing? *I'm going to write songs for that Amati voice. I might even run my fingers through that hair.*

The assembly popped the bubble with a breathy exhalation and then burst into applause. Brahms glanced at Clara's conflicted face. Her mind was in ferment: a single song of her late husband's had cracked the special bond with the young genius Robert had adored, and whom she adored still. All because of a pretty voice.

She stood up. 'My apologies, everyone,' she stammered. 'Will you excuse me? I must see to the children.' A swish of her black dress and she left the room.

Julius looked on with concern. 'Pine – could you ... ?' he said, nodding in the direction of the creaking footsteps on the stairs.

'Of course, Ise. I'll be back soon, everyone.' She left in pursuit of their guest.

Clapping his hands, Grimm said, 'Now, Johannes. Who's next?'

Brahms stood, looking again at Agathe. 'No one else for now,' he said. 'Let's have some choruses, yes? A cappella.'

~

For the first time in his life that he could recall, Johannes felt his own age. He'd been a serious old man ever since childhood, he realised, lost in his books and dreams. His youth had died two years before while he watched the pathetic spectacle of the deranged Schumann sucking drops of wine from Clara's finger during his last days on earth.

Now, in the summer of his twenty-sixth year, Brahms allowed Life to seduce him with the peace and green of the forests, the warmth of summer air, the laughter of others, the sense of a beginning, and above all, a young woman he wanted. He wrote songs for her when he knew he should have been polishing up the first movement of the concerto that was supposed to announce his genius to the world the following January. The 'dutiful' Johannes whispered this in his ear at night while he imagined peeling the dress from Agathe's ripe body.

Well, dutiful Johannes could be damned for a precious few weeks. Instead, he would play games. The more childish, the better.

'Hide-and-seek, everyone?' asked Agathe's friend Bertha one afternoon. 'There's an allotment nearby where anyone can disappear.'

Clara wanted to come too.

'Don't you think she's a bit ... *old* for this?' said Bertha's boyfriend, Heinrich. 'What I mean is – black's a bit of a giveaway.'

Johannes stayed loyal. 'If *she's* too old for this, so are *we.* Strictly speaking, the cut-off date for infantile pursuits is when one stops being an infant.'

'Hey, I'm only saying . . .' said Heinrich. He wasn't going to argue with the season's golden boy.

Someone noticed a flash of black near an asparagus bed. 'I see you!' he yelled.

Clara hoisted her dress and began the sprint for home through the paths between the plantings. It was the first time Johannes had ever heard her giggle.

The ground was uneven. She tripped over a large tree root at the allotment exit and fell to the ground in a cascade of fabric.

The others stood aghast. It was fine for *them* to take a tumble; somehow anyone even slightly older having the same accident looked embarrassingly infirm. Brahms was the first to reach her. She was fine, but he insisted on taking her back to the Grimms' house while the others continued their game.

'I just didn't know it was there, Johannes,' she said, recovering her breath. There was something so poignant in her voice that a tear sprang to his eye. Pity widened the emerging gap between them.

'Think nothing of it, my dear, dear one. Silly game.'

That evening was a special one in Julius's parlour. Johannes had written some songs and duets, and Agathe would sing them.

'What are we to hear?' Pine asked the pair. Brahms stood formally behind the keyboard.

'Friends – this is a setting of a poem from last century by Hölty. It's called – "The Kiss".'

'I wonder what gave him that idea,' somebody whispered. A ripple of giggles spread through the gathering. The song told of flirtation, hand-holding and lips meeting for the first time. It was over in little more than a minute.

Bertha looked at Heinrich during the applause.

'Very *sombre*, isn't it?' she said. 'You'd think he'd sound happier.'

'Doesn't sound to me like they've kissed at all,' he replied.

Brahms stood again. 'The next one is a poem by Uhland: "Parting and Separation".'

Julius turned to his wife. 'I'm not sure I know where this is going,' he said.

The song was shorter than the first. When they had finished, Agathe looked at Johannes with undisguised affection. She was glowing.

'They look so happy together,' Pine said. She looked back at Clara, who was staring at the floor, and nudged her husband. 'This must be terrible for Clara, Julius. Can we change the mood?'

Grimm jumped up. 'Thank you both for those two premieres,' he said. 'Johannes, what about a party piece? One of those Hungarian encores that are making you famous?'

Brahms nodded with an approving smirk. 'The ersatz gypsy music, you mean? What a fortuitous suggestion, Ise. They're mostly arrangements of old tunes, but lately I've been tinkering with a completely original one in the gypsy style. Shall I?'

He swivelled back to the keyboard. 'I'd like to dedicate this rendition to the spirit of Amati. Imagine the great Joachim here with us, singing this on his violin.'

Brahms more than made up for Joachim's absence, managing both the fiddle tune and the striding accompaniment, his hands ranging deftly around the keys. The song was full of yearning, pulling at the hearts of everyone.

Agathe looked at the young face transfixed by the slow-burning passion in the music. She discerned a note of regret in its melodies, remembering what Grimm had said when he first suggested she and Brahms meet: 'Johannes has every reason to be happy about what will come to him, dear girl. But that's not an indulgence he usually grants himself. We will have to *show* him how to be happy.'

SEPTEMBER

Summer raced towards its close.

The revellers had walked through a nearby forest late one afternoon to watch the twilight fall through a canopy of leaves showing the first tints of autumn, and began to make their way back to the Grimms' for an early-evening drink.

Agathe tugged at Brahms's arm. 'Johannes, we can take our time,' she said.

They fell back as the others pushed ahead.

'It's very comfortable like this,' he said, relishing the slight pressure of her breast against him as they drew close against the chill. 'I could imagine it being even more comfortable.'

'Me too,' she said. For all their closeness over the past months, conversation had been strangely decorous, as if Johannes was always checking himself from saying what he wanted – or perhaps, trying to decide what he *did* want. As soon as the subject turned to music he became so animated, looking so beautiful with his face lit up, it was all she could do not to invite him to kiss her as hard as she would like, to let her hands explore him. He remained an obstinate mystery to her, apart from what she could divine from his songs. Everything he had written for her that summer spoke of love. With Johannes, the music did the talking.

She noticed some bushes by the path.

'Come with me, Johannes,' she whispered urgently, pulling him behind the shrubbery, hiding them from view.

He looked nervous. Not nervous enough to try to leave.

'Johannes,' she said, her face close, her breath warm on his cheeks, 'you'll be gone soon to prepare for the next phase of your life. Your concerto will be heard by the elite crowd in Leipzig. It'll be a success, I know. What you've played to me is gigantic and wonderful.'

He felt aroused as she snuggled against him.

'I have just one question,' she continued. 'Is that *all* there will be in the next phase of your life?'

The summer was always going to come to this moment, he realised: the moment when lust would have to be dealt with. Johannes wasn't happy with lust's encroachment into his friendships with women. He always went to prostitutes when he needed relief. *Sure, you need relief at times*, he said to himself, *you're young.* The problem was that he couldn't imagine sleeping with someone he loved; it was the conclusion he'd come to with Clara. And since he wasn't even sure if he could love at all, it was better to assign carnality to the same category of needs as food and drink, so that love had nothing to do with it. *You don't love the loaf of bread before you cut it up.*

He knew he'd been cursed by the things he'd seen as a child, playing piano in some of those hideous places on the Hamburg docks, watching with horror the things men did to women, loathing the way women gave themselves away like that. He'd never been able to exalt love in the manner of the poets; if he tried, he would only make a fool of himself.

Flushed with wine one night he'd said to Joachim, 'Jussuf, I can't love an unmarried girl.'

'That's a problem,' Joachim had said. 'What about a married one?'

'*Married?* What sort of person do you think I am? That's out of the question.' *Even if she's married to me, I suspect.*

There was no need to explain this to Agathe right now. She was a good Catholic and had sufficient strength of will not to compromise herself. That, no doubt, was why she asked him the question. He had asked himself the same. *What next?*

She couldn't stop her face pressing nearer in the dusk, closing her lips over his, not releasing, feeling the heat rising in his cheeks, his tongue in her mouth . . .

'*Oh.* Oh. I'm s-s-sorry.'

It was Clara.

'I-I wondered what had happened when I couldn't find you in the group, Johannes, and then I heard your voices. And, and – *please* excuse me.' She stepped away and walked quickly in the direction of the house.

'Go *after* her, Johannes!' Agathe said. Grimm had told her something of the complex history with Clara.

'Tomorrow,' he said. *Can't you see that any attempt at consolation would be even more humiliating for her?*

He called at the Grimms' late the next morning, steeled for a heart-to-heart.

'You're too late, Johannes,' Julius said. 'Clara's gone.'

'I'll wait until she returns, Ise. How long do you think she'll be?'

'You don't understand, Johannes. Clara has taken the children and left Göttingen. Her holiday is over.'

LEIPZIG, 27 JANUARY 1859

Flexing his fingers, Brahms scanned the faces of the audience in the Gewandhaus while the orchestra tuned up.

The most important day of his life so far, and Clara hadn't come.

It wasn't surprising. Much as he and Agathe had wanted to keep their engagement a secret, word was bound to get out. Julius and Pine had probably guessed when they saw the rings on her and Johannes's fingers. And it *was* Julius's suggestion.

'People are talking, Johannes, especially after that final episode with Clara, and Göttingen's a small place. Gathe's a wonderful girl, but she'll be humiliated around town if you don't do the right thing by her with all that's happened. You clearly adore each other. Why don't you take the plunge? It's what we all expect.'

Why not, indeed? Johannes had missed Agathe terribly during those few months in Detmold while he prepared for the concerto's performances. He'd written her songs and letters. He'd dreamed of that dark hair spread across a bedsheet, the curves of her plush body finally available to him on the night of their wedding. He'd even tried his hand at writing a bridal song, but the result was so dull he suppressed it. Instead, he composed a funeral song. *That* had come out much better.

He decided Agathe was the one to banish his demons once and for all, that Julius's advice should be heeded. Earlier that month, he'd returned to Göttingen for the first time since the previous summer.

'Agathe, we were going to make a quartet from your trio with Ise and Gur. Did we succeed?' he said.

She lifted her face from the cluster of welts she was making on his neck.

'Darling Johannes, even three was a crowd.'

Brahms thought he might explode with desire, but the die was cast: he would avoid visiting his favourite whores and wait for satisfaction until his marriage. The heaviness was not only in his heart when he travelled to Hanover for the concerto's first public outing.

It hadn't gone well. The public expected some highwire brilliance and joie de vivre from Germany's most stunning musical prospect since Beethoven. But Brahms disappointed them. He'd struggled mightily to get that first movement on paper, and the struggle was there to hear in the explosive opening, engulfing the audience straight away, picking up where the dramatic end of the first movement of Beethoven's Ninth left off, right down to the same key signature. After the prolonged cataclysm, it was hard for the remainder of the concerto to pick up the pieces. The reception was confused. It felt trite to congratulate soldiers for having fought a war.

But that was Hanover. Leipzig was an entirely different matter. *This* was the performance that counted.

The piano was rolled into place in front of the orchestra, the tuning completed.

'You may proceed, maestro,' said the stage manager.

Johannes walked onstage to tepid applause. He knew that neither the orchestra nor the conductor, Rietz, liked his piece. Had they told others? Naturally.

He bowed and made one last attempt to find those familiar dark-blue eyes in the front row.

They weren't there.

The timpanist pounded the concerto into life, its D minor tonality veering off-course almost immediately. He saw some of the older audience members jerk their heads back, recoiling at the violence.

The first movement's assault lasted for nearly twenty-five minutes, a minute for every year of his life. It felt like the *story* of his life. He was centre-stage, playing his own tumultuous history, baring every corner of his soul.

It was the custom to applaud between movements. He expected a hail of bravos for his honesty after such a convulsive confession. The movement thundered out the final bars, and the composer lifted his arms from the keyboard in a grand gesture as the conductor sliced off the last chord.

Nothing, apart from the clearing of a few throats.

Rietz looked at Brahms as if to say: *You see? They agree with me. This really is shit.*

When the second movement began with orchestra alone, Brahms wished more than ever for Clara's presence. This part of the concerto was her portrait, the expression of feelings for her he'd never been able to put properly into words. She was still the person whose praise and advice meant the most to him. Pure, virginal Clara – that is how he would always regard her.

The silence of the audience at the movement's end, punctuated by shuffling and whispering, signalled the end of the battle. The finale that followed was dwarfed by all that had gone before; its grasp at swagger in the theme rang hollow, the switch to major tonality at the end not the victory lap he'd hoped for. He was relieved when it was over. It had been a gruelling three-quarters of an hour. *Nobody* wrote concertos that long. Surely this crowd would recognise the magnitude of what they'd just heard?

There was a pause while the last note echoed down the hall.

Very slowly, three pairs of hands clapped in the very back row. A slow clap of derision. The rest of the audience hissed like snakes. Brahms bowed stiffly and walked off the platform, the hisses continuing until he was out of sight. He didn't return for a second bow.

Watching the grisly spectacle, the music critic for the Leipzig *Signale* newspaper turned to his wife and said, 'It's always unpleasant to see a new work being taken to its grave.'

～

Back in his room, Brahms removed his hat, dress coat and gloves and threw them on the bed. A table near the window bore the heavy manuscript of the Piano Concerto No 1.

He looked at those familiar pages. Nearly five years' work leading up to that night, and with more to come – *if* the concerto was to survive at all.

If he could be bothered.

Then again, shouldn't he be feeling worse than this? After such opprobrium, being fed to the lion of an ignorant public? Johannes would have been justified in taking up residence at the nearest bar to drown his sorrows. Instead, he'd been almost whistling as he climbed the stairs just now.

He sat at the table and opened his score, flipping idly through the first few dozen pages, remembering the thought and sweat that had gone into every familiar bar; the crossings-out, the rewrites, the marginalia. He'd have to write to Joachim tomorrow to tell his side of the story while his friend read the reviews. *Dear God* – what those reviews would be like.

His mind was clear. What could he learn from this disaster?

First, most importantly: he was three-quarters of the way there with the piece, still feeling his way in some matters of structure and orchestration. They were nothing that further revisions couldn't improve. The performance's failure that night was the fault of the *audience*; not the work, not his playing or that of the orchestra. Most of the players hadn't liked the piece either, but they'd done an excellent job by him. That unhelpful arsehole Rietz on the podium was of no consequence. Lesson One.

Following on from that, Johannes had to be realistic about his immediate prospects: itinerancy and comparative poverty would be a part of his circumstances for some time yet. He'd have to go back to Hamburg and live with his parents until he could afford a place of his own and make a stable base. Supporting himself would be hard enough, without the burden of trying to support *someone else*. Lesson Two.

Which led him to Lesson Three.

Agathe.

He understood now why he was taking the events of the night so well.

Because I don't have to explain this to anyone.

He imagined Agathe – *any* wife – at home, waiting to support him in his adversity, to comfort him, tell him that it would all be better next time.

To *pity* him.

She couldn't understand that he wasn't unhappy about this, nor that an artist like him might have a vision that continued to burn bright despite her empty, consoling words. She would feel and look concerned, thinking it a problem shared.

What a hell that would be. A hell in chains: *Marriage*.

He couldn't stand it. Not now, not ever.

Agathe would have to be told. He'd write a letter. Somehow, he'd try to make it as light as possible to lessen the blow; insouciant and breezy – everything the First Piano Concerto wasn't.

Now was as good a time as ever. Johannes grabbed a pen and a sheet of clean paper, and began writing.

'*My dearest Agathe! I love you, and I must see you again! But . . .*'
And so on.

Two hours later, the lamp in his room burning low, the chill of the winter night leaking in through the window glazing, Brahms signed his first name, sealed the completed letter in an envelope and wrote her name on the front.

He suspected the letter's tone was not its strong suit and wondered if its sum effect would be as disastrous as that night's concert. Agathe's reaction was hard for him to predict; the Grimms' less so. He could imagine what Julius would say. Johannes felt much the same himself.

He pressed the palms of his tired hands against his eyes and said aloud: 'Johannes Brahms – you are a fucking scoundrel.'

POSTSCRIPT

Agathe von Siebold replied to Brahms's letter by breaking off the engagement and returning his ring. They never saw each other again. Likewise, Julius Grimm and his wife severed all contact with the composer.

Agathe spent several more years in Göttingen before leaving Germany to become a governess in Ireland. She finally married ten years after the rupture with her former fiancé.

Brahms's First Piano Concerto was performed in Hamburg in March 1859, two months after the Leipzig disaster. This time it was a huge success, launching the composer's career. A subsequent Hamburg performance in 1861, conducted by Brahms, featured Clara Schumann as soloist.

Brahms and Clara Schumann remained close until her death in May 1896. Brahms died less than a year later.

THE UNKNOWN ISLAND

Love was always essential to Hector Berlioz: the only
other preoccupation of his life apart from music, and
the inspiration for much of his work. A brief episode
in the sunset of his years became the purest of his
romantic episodes, teaching the composer that age
was not necessarily the end.

~

'A love came to me, smiling. I did not seek it and even resisted for a
time, but this inexorable need of tenderness overcame me. I let myself
be loved. Then I myself loved even more.'

Hector Berlioz, letter to Humbert Ferrand, 3 March 1863

PARIS, 1862

'Monsieur! Your handkerchief!'

She walked quickly towards him along a path lined with
gravestones, her hand outstretched.

His face still streaked with tears, Hector Berlioz felt embarrassed to be identified as the owner of the mislaid item.

'Merci, mademoiselle,' he said before noticing the ring on her finger. 'Pardon me – *madame*.'

Her chestnut hair was parted in the middle and gathered at the back of her head by side braids. Very à la mode, he guessed – as one might expect from a well-kept married woman who looked to be only in her twenties.

She had noticed him weeping long before he began to move on from the gravesite where his handkerchief had fallen to the ground. He made a striking sight; fine-checked trousers and well-cut grey long coat with an upturned fawn collar, sheathing a slender, still youthful figure. Even without the decoration of tears, anyone's attention would have been drawn to the head designed in antiquity: an aquiline, beak-like nose, deep-set eyes shining below a broad expanse of forehead. And his hair! Even in his youth, friends had described the almost comically abundant reddish-blond thatch as 'a forest tumbling over the edge of a precipice'. Age had changed its colour, but not its density.

All Berlioz saw in his mirror each day was the whitening hair of age, and this sudden apparition of youth in a cemetery made him feel even older. The pains that had kept him awake the night before flared again. He winced, placing his hands over his stomach.

'Are you all right, monsieur?' she said, concerned.

'Ah! My neuralgia,' he said, through shortened breath. 'The affliction of my years.'

'Perhaps you will allow me to help you to a bench.'

He was not altogether happy about the spectacle of his

infirmity requiring such public assistance. A moment later he realised there was little point in feeling self-conscious when surrounded by people whose views were obscured by six feet of earth.

It was a fine day for late autumn. The trees in Montmartre Cemetery were more alive than its inhabitants, and bouquets placed on the graves lent an almost festive look to what he called the 'charnel house'. The irony was not lost on Berlioz that lingering here was a less depressing prospect than mouldering at home.

'That would be a benefit, madame,' he said, 'much more comfortable than the last time I felt this way while here. Then, I had to lie on a tombstone for hours.'

Besides, she really was quite beautiful, he thought. Berlioz was reassured to notice there was more curiosity than pity in her eyes. Or was he just being fanciful?

Of course I am, he thought. *That's how artists are. We conjure fancies for a meagre living. This sweet girl is helping an afflicted old man in a graveyard.*

'And the name of this kind stranger would be. . . ?' He waited for her to complete his sentence.

The informality of her reply was a surprise.

'Amélie,' she said. 'The rest is of no importance.'

'I shall give you mine in case you need to seek help,' he said, half in earnest. 'I am Monsieur Berlioz. My apartment is not far from here, in the rue de Calais.'

'Berlioz . . . I know your name. I have *seen* it,' she said. 'Of course! The *Journal des débats*. You are the music critic?'

'Paris is not a city crowded with people bearing my name.

You are indeed correct, madame – although you know me only for what I do for a living, not for who I was.'

She did not detect the deliberate irony in his remark.

'And that would be?'

'I was condemned by Fate to be a composer of music,' he said with faux theatricality. 'Paris, in her wisdom, ensured that news of this was not spread throughout the land.'

Amélie wasn't sure whether she was meant to feel complicit in the scale of such public ignorance. Then she was aware of his sideways glance through what she now saw to be blue-grey eyes, and the beginning of a smile on lips no longer tightened by pain.

'I presume you are not here today merely to mourn your reputation, monsieur,' she teased.

'All of those tears were shed long ago, Madame Amélie. The resurrection of that particular corpse is a hundred years away. No – today I weep as we all do who visit. Too much of my past is beneath this earth. I once wrote a song about it in a cycle about the loss of love. The singer is in a cemetery by moonlight, hearing a dove above a white tomb. The ghost of his lover asks if he will come back to her grave, but he knows he will not.'

'Since you are here, you are clearly not he,' she said.

'I have not such strength of character.'

'Shedding tears for the dead is not a sign of weakness, Monsieur Berlioz,' she said gently. 'What is your cycle called? Perhaps I should find your music.'

'*Summer Nights*,' he said. 'I wrote it twenty years ago, before I had any friends in this place. The music in that song captures exactly the exhaustion with life I now feel. How could I have known of it then? All I did was to imagine what it might be like.

Experience teaches us nothing new; it only confirms the direst predictions of youth.'

'Then I have a great deal in which to look forward, for none of my predictions are so dire,' she said. 'And not all of yours are correct, monsieur. You look much better than you did a few minutes ago.'

'That's because I have encountered life and beauty in a place where it was least expected. Do not blush, madame; I say that with the sagacity of the old.'

She looked at him. 'You are not old, Monsieur Berlioz. You are simply more experienced. I should like to hear more about those experiences that have left you so innocent of knowledge.'

~

They spent a further hour at the cemetery, exchanging platitudes about the state of the world. When she suggested that the approaching winter would only make both the trees around them and any further platitudes more funereal, Berlioz invited her to meet him again the next week in the warmth of the Café Le Cardinal on the corner of rue de Richelieu and the boulevard des Italiens, where conversation could outlast the light of the afternoons.

'I pretend that it is convenient – and it is. I live around the corner,' Berlioz admitted after greeting her at a table by the window. 'The real reason is that of sentiment; I have been coming here for nearly forty years. You remember, don't you, *mon vieux?*' he called to the old *patron* presiding at the bar.

'How could one forget, Monsieur Berlioz? It must have been 1827? '28? You came in one night looking very upset and then collapsed on the table over there. Nobody was game to approach in case you had died. You slept there for most of the night.'

'I was probably about your age, Amélie,' said Berlioz. 'I had spent the entire day and much of the night wandering around the city and surrounding plain. Montmartre was a hamlet on the edge of the country in those days.'

'Too much exercise, monsieur?' she said.

'No, madame: too much passion – always being in love.'

'Unhappy songs, tears in a cemetery, fainting in cafés; love seems to bring you much grief.'

'It has brought me a great deal of music, and a wonderful son, Louis, whom I see too rarely. Music and love are the two wings of the soul.'

Amélie remembered the hurt creature she had first seen. *He is nursing a broken wing*, she thought. He was a sad, earthbound eagle – but at least he had flown. She had not, she convinced herself – not yet in her short life, anyway.

'Monsieur Berlioz, I cannot speak for music, but in my limited experience love offers no guarantee of happiness,' she said. It was a second before she realised what a self-revealing comment she had made.

He looked at her keenly, just as surprised. Her face had the same neutral expression as if she'd remarked on the colour of the tablecloth, but her voice betrayed cynicism, rather than melancholy. As indispensible as love had been in his own life, Berlioz had come to exactly the same conclusion as the one Amélie had just voiced. Yet he would never be cynical about it. That was the difference between their generations: his had discovered Beethoven and Shakespeare; hers danced the cancan.

Perhaps not *her*, though. He felt that she was a kindred spirit.

He looked out into the street. People were emerging from so many more carriages than before, shoulders hunched against the cold, some of them coming into the Cardinal, which had been made into something more respectable than in the old days when he slumped over the furniture.

All was change. The newly installed gas lamps were just being lit, bringing day to night in a way he had never known when he was young. Baron Haussmann's new boulevards were gouging their way through his neighbourhood. Not that he minded; he liked the new aesthetic. But there were inconveniences. Even the dead had to make way for the 'new' Paris; soon, his first wife would have to be disinterred.

Whichever way Berlioz looked at it, the past was being dug up. He had even dredged up his own and written it down in his memoirs. Would the young woman sitting in front of him ever read them? If she did, would she care? Something in him suddenly wanted her to *care*.

The lessons of his life might be instructive. This new acquaintance from the cemetery sounded as if she needed her cynicism put to bed for a few decades. She could always be old and bitter later.

His decision took only a few seconds. Then he drew himself up, brightening his voice.

'I want to make a suggestion to you, Madame Amélie. If it sounds too generous, be assured that the person who will benefit most is myself. On the other hand, the thought of it may bore you to tears – but you did invite me last week to tell you something about my "experiences".'

'Monsieur Berlioz, I cannot imagine being bored in the slightest,' she said, smiling. 'Tell me your idea.'

'I would like to tell you what I know of love, Amélie. It's an unlikely novel that spans my life, but to prevent it becoming the ramblings of an old man I'll confine it to those parts that eventually made their way into my music. And should you ever *hear* my music someday, you will then have the dubious privilege of knowing me completely. We could have some tisane as an accompaniment. Do you have the inclination – and the time?'

'I am inclined to hear whatever you wish to say, Monsieur Berlioz,' she said. 'And my husband is always away, so I have all the time in the world.'

'You will need it. My son is at sea for his profession, and we shall take a voyage too. Let us have the wind at our backs. We are setting sail for a place that may not exist.'

'What is its name, monsieur?'

'The place where love lasts forever,' he said.

～

Berlioz talked into that evening and through more weekly meetings, confessing more to this unusual young woman than he did to many of his friends. The ones who lived nearby kept an open door for Hector Berlioz; he would sometimes arrive unannounced and sit by their fires, saying nothing apart from the usual niceties. When he was in a better mood, he would fire bon mots over dinner, or talk sagely to their grandchildren. *Handle Hector with care*, they counselled each other; he was recently widowed for a second time, he was unsettled, his belongings had been moved to a lower floor of his apartment block while repairs were being made to the building.

The Opéra had just rejected his huge opera *The Trojans* that he talked about as the crowning achievement of his creative life. He still worked in a job he detested, writing about music he knew to be not a patch on his own, and the mysterious illness in his guts was pulling him down inch by inch. There were plenty of reasons for him to carry a handkerchief, even if he wasn't visiting a grave.

At least his new opera based on his beloved Shakespeare's *Much Ado About Nothing* had been a success recently in Baden, where the wealthy took a break from the gambling tables and spa baths to talk through, and then applaud, what he called his 'caprice written with the point of a needle'. He knew it would be his last work, and after all the unhappiness in his life, he intended to go out with a smile.

His musical labours over, he now had an audience more available than any his Trojans might have delivered him, more attentive than the socialites and gamblers of Baden. On her part, Amélie was happy to be a captive, too enthralled by both the stories and the raconteur to leave.

Berlioz alluded to his age as the excuse for any unintended mistakes when finishing another tale: 'Of course I *would* say that now – I am almost fifty-nine!' She found the mantra increasingly hard to believe. His animated facial expressions, the precise movements of the hands that had made him such a renowned conductor of orchestras, and the way in which he would flick back his extravagant hair when it threatened to lose control were all the traits of a much younger man.

The stories of love began with his first, in 1816. Her name

was Stella – his 'star' – and she wore pink boots. He was twelve, blushing furiously, staring at those boots in a crowded room in country France, and if he looked up into the eyes of the person wearing them he knew he would swoon.

He was already prone to being overwhelmed by music, scenery and the romance of antiquity. The sound of plainchant by a distant congregation would send him rolling around the nearest hill in agony, and the vision of poor Dido on her funeral pyre in Virgil's *Aeneid* caused him to stammer and fall silent during a Latin lesson with his father. Berlioz senior was a good country doctor, but even without such medical insights he knew his firstborn was a most unusual child.

Estelle's family were friends of his grandfather, who the Berlioz family visited each summer. From his village above the Isère Valley near Grenoble you could see the jagged horizon of mountaintops marching away to the Alps.

It was the perfect setting in which to be smitten by the sight of a beautiful young woman standing on a rock during a mountainside ramble on a warm afternoon. There she was, admiring the view, a mythological figurehead with her black hair streaming in the light wind, the cliffs of Meylan behind her. She was eighteen.

A boy fell in love for his first time – with an older woman. Of course, it was more than hopeless; it was the object of fun at a social dance gathering.

'I couldn't speak; it would have betrayed the immensity of my feelings to the room,' Berlioz said. 'Later, I thought I would write an opera for her and leave it on that rock for her to discover one morning. Crazy, of course, but you know, I still might do it someday. There isn't a month that I don't think of her. In her way, she is my most sacred memory. I'm told she married and enjoys a life without drama. It must be wonderful.'

'I can assure you it is not, Monsieur Berlioz,' said Amélie, cradling her tea with both hands, avoiding his eyes. 'You make drama sound like something essential to life.'

'Most drama in life is best avoided, madame. So much of it is unnecessary. I can think of only one exception in my own case. That's why I call it the supreme drama of my life.'

He took his story forward to 1827, when a troupe of actors from across the Channel gave a season of Shakespeare at the Odéon Theatre in Paris. All were English, save one player from Ireland, Harriet Smithson, who took on the leading roles in *Hamlet* and *Romeo and Juliet*. The young Berlioz attended the opening night, together with those who would become famous as the French 'Romantics', none of them able to understand a word of English, all of them thunderstruck by the experience.

'It wasn't just Harriet's acting genius – yes, it *was* genius in the way she played Ophelia, tearing me apart with her voice and gestures – there was the revelation of Shakespeare as well,' he said. 'Harriet brought me to the light. I chose to love the messenger.'

His subsequent behaviour became the talk of Paris: the abject letters to the actress who cautioned her circle to 'beware the gentleman with the eyes that bode no good', the letters to his friends, the sleepless nights on nocturnal walks ending in collapses in ditches or cafés like the Cardinal – the paroxysms of a young man taken to the edge of insanity by an obsession lasting days and nights for over two years. At the end of it all, he had a symphony, his 'Episode in the Life of an Artist' – the *Fantastic Symphony*.

'How does someone who is close to madness create something so coherent?' said Amélie, astonished.

'Like all mad artists?' he said with a grin. 'That's the legend, isn't it – the crazed genius in the garret? Passion is not as debilitating as you think, Amélie. I transferred my state of mind and all my malignant impulses to paper, leaving my mind clear. The young artist at the centre of its story does all the things I could never have done, even at my nadir; it starts with a failed suicide and goes downhill from there. I even wrote a description of what the music is about. Harriet is there all the way through, a recurring melody, a fixed idea – all the way to the witches' dance at the end.'

'I'm sure she was delighted about that,' said Amélie, grinning in turn.

'She didn't know – we'd never met, and I moved on for a while to someone else,' said Berlioz. His vagueness was intentional. 'It's liberating, becoming a voyeur of one's own life. For me, to be creative is to be at a remove from the enslavement of feeling. I told Wagner I could only draw the moon by seeing its reflection at the bottom of a well.'

Amélie looked puzzled. 'That sounds cold, Monsieur Berlioz. I remember the man I first saw in a cemetery a few weeks ago. He was not without feeling.'

He felt for the presence of his handkerchief.

'Now, in my dotage, I do not create. All that space in my life where music used to be! Once again, it is filled with too many feelings, but they are only old ones, bringing all of my past back with them. I suppose this is the nostalgia of the elderly,' he said, more to himself than to her.

'Perhaps it is time you created some new ones,' she said.

'When I am here with you, such a thing seems possible,' he said.

She blushed, and moved back to Berlioz's story. 'What happened to Miss Smithson?'

'Oh, it ended badly. She became Madame Berlioz.'

'*What?*' said Amélie, incredulous.

Berlioz traced the trajectory of a love first incarnated in music as it spiralled down once life stepped in. Harriet finally heard the *Fantastic Symphony* two years after it was written; its public status as a love letter made a formal meeting unavoidable. She capitulated, they exchanged expressions of love in fractured versions of each other's language, married against the opposition of his parents, had a son and struggled with finances as his career went up and hers went down, taking her looks and self-esteem with it. She hit the bottle, and the drinking stoked the fire of suspicion; midnight demands that he swear to his fidelity, he protesting his innocence.

And through all that decade of the 1830s, some of his greatest music: an opera about Benvenuto Cellini, a massive Requiem with its Day of Judgement, and three more symphonies, including one where Harriet's light shone one last glorious time – *Romeo and Juliet*, with a love scene in the garden of the Capulets that he always thought to be the most beautiful music he ever wrote.

'Looking back, it was my farewell to Harriet, my tribute to the dawn of that love,' he said sadly. 'Music can give an idea of love. It doesn't seem to work the other way around.'

He stopped at that point. Was it propriety or cowardice that made him unwilling to describe an ending that lacked any of the poetry of a beginning? Having a mistress was not uncommon in Paris, but abandoning one's wife for one was a vulgar turn of events for someone of Berlioz's supposed refinement of character. It didn't feel very romantic in real life when he eloped with a singer whose dubious vocal talents were easily eclipsed by those she showed in bed, and it didn't feel very poetic when Marie turned up on Harriet's doorstep one day to announce herself as the 'preferred' Madame Berlioz. It wasn't beautiful to observe Harriet's descent through alcoholism and strokes to her death in 1854. None of this sounded like the stuff of a romantic symphony.

The only way to atone for more than a decade of moral dishonour was to make his mistress a 'respectable' woman. Sure, it was not love any more – it never really had been, he had to admit – but at least the ménage promised him some stability for the rest of his life; and besides, his Spanish mother-in-law was totally devoted to him.

But just as love had shown no longevity, neither had pragmatism.

'That is why we met where we did, madame,' Berlioz said. 'My wife died earlier this year. A heart attack; she was not yet fifty.'

Amélie was dumbstruck. 'You say you did not love her as you did Harriet, and yet you can weep by her grave?'

'Amélie, think back to our very first conversation, when I mentioned the lessons of experience and talked about my song cycle *Summer Nights*.'

'The ghost of the lover?'

'That's right. The cycle ends with a song called "The Unknown Island". A young girl asks a boatman to take her to the shore where love lasts forever. He replies casually that nobody knows where that is, *ma chère*. How about we try for someplace else? I place a little minor cadence at that point to give it a mock-serious tone, like a half-hearted eulogy at a funeral. Twenty years later, I weep in a cemetery because time proved that boatman right.'

There was an awkward silence. Amélie reached for his hand to anticipate the tears that might follow. That was the excuse she gave herself, anyway.

'That's not necessarily the right deduction, monsieur,' she said. 'Perhaps he was always sailing in the wrong direction. It happens, you know. We all live in hope for some better navigation. Haven't you wondered why I happened to be in Montmartre Cemetery at the same time as you that day?'

His face relaxed as his eyes widened in amazement at his own lack of curiosity.

'It has never occurred to me, madame. A pleasant walk to pass the time? You said your husband is always away.'

'Indeed he is, Monsieur Berlioz. He died last year. I too was visiting a grave.'

Now it was Berlioz's turn to open his mouth in disbelief. 'I saw your ring, but you were not wearing black.'

'One only mourns the passing of those whom one has loved,' she said.

Things changed rapidly between Berlioz and his café confidante after that.

Amélie had become a student of his life. He felt she had already intuited as many things about living as he had actually lived. With such an even level of exchange their bond deepened: soon he was 'Hector', and very soon after that, 'dear Hector'. They both pretended these were merely expressions of complicity.

They took walks together, he leaning against her for support and a little warmth, she snuggling her left hand into the wide sleeve of his coat. Her body felt thin as it pressed against his. They were both glad that winter's cold gave them an excuse for closeness.

One morning they returned arm in arm to the cemetery where it all began. Amélie took Hector to her husband's grave, the headstone still new and gleaming white. She spoke little about him, except to remark that she had been very young, and he a much older man.

Berlioz looked at her, an eyebrow raised.

She actually laughed – her husband lying just there – and said, 'No, my dear Hector, even then it was never love's dream! I have been ill for much of my life and he promised my parents to look after me no matter what might come. It was accepted on all sides as an arrangement.'

Then they moved on like a pair of official greeters to search out the other new arrivals, the flowers still fresh on the cold stone.

When Amélie stopped unexpectedly one morning in that place of death, held his face, kissed him, and drew away while whispering 'my dear Hector', he looked around for witnesses. The winter was not the culprit *this* time.

'Sweet Amélie . . .' he began, pausing to be interrupted because he did not know what else to say.

'Hector, I want your boatman to be wrong,' she said.

That evening she came to his apartment. His mother-in-law had stayed on after her daughter's death to look after the widowed composer, but she was away.

Amélie asked to stay, and they lay down together fully dressed on his bed for the entire night, he wanting only to hold her to him as she slept. When he woke the next morning she had left. Her short letter was on a side table, written in a firm hand.

My dearest friend
I see land ahead. Come ashore with me.
Then I might hear your music.
Who can say how much time we have?
You are loved.
Your Amélie

The love scene of his Romeo and Juliet symphony came to his mind, with the cellos in the orchestra capturing all the ardour of the young Montague with the first appearance of their soaring theme, and in comparing it with this, the first simple declaration of love he had ever received in his life, Berlioz realised that once again his music had anticipated the reality.

By the time he showed the letter to his friend Legouvé, he had already decided how this should play out, even though he loved her in return. As much as she insisted that the difference in their ages had no bearing on her feelings, a voice of pessimism or pragmatism from the depths of his heart kept on reminding him that this love was impossible.

'I'm sixty, Ernest,' he said. 'Look at these wrinkles.'

'What does that matter if she sees you as thirty?' said Legouvé. 'Wrinkles don't matter in someone like you. She is a superior woman, full of warmth and tenderness. You don't think she can assess the risk?'

'She cannot love me. My friend, this is a heaven I must not enter – for her sake.'

And then he sobbed inconsolably. So did Amélie when Berlioz told her.

∼

They saw each other once more, at a performance of his opera *The Trojans*, picked up by the impresario Carvalho and staged at the Théâtre-Lyrique in November the following year in a stunted version.

Amélie was standing with an older woman across the crowded lobby during an interval, her eyes boring into him through a wall of Second Empire finery. She looked tired, thinner than when he explained to her on a shiny spring afternoon why they should not meet again. When she stepped away from her escort, making a space that he was being invited to fill, he resisted the impulse and instead nodded his greeting. Her face sagged and she nodded back, before their sightlines were obscured by the crush of patrons returning to their seats to watch Aeneas rush off to Rome, leaving Dido behind to kill herself.

PARIS, 1864

Hector Berlioz paid his respects to his two wives, noticing that Harriet's grave was less well-tended than Marie's; his mother-in-law was dedicated to the neat preservation of her daughter's memory. He would bring his first wife some more fresh flowers next time.

Remembering the walks he used to take around the cemetery in company during those magical winter days, he thought he would look for the new headstones and their unfortunate subjects. He felt complicity with them now. They were just a little way up the queue from him, if his worsening gut was any indication.

The terrain was so familiar, its alternation of black and white marble, gilt lettering and simple carving, the florid and the austere, all burned into his memory. One headstone over to his left had something about it he remembered less well . . . of *course*, it was that of Amélie's husband; her unloved protector, the person described by his widow in a café as being 'away all the time'.

Berlioz stepped over to inspect the grave for only the second time, curious to see how the passage of time had worked its way into the stone. Its pristine whiteness had faded, the formerly clean edges of the carving already showing the first signs of their inevitable obliteration. The stone alongside was newer still, ready to endure the onslaught of a harsh Parisian winter. He leaned closer to check the dates.

Then he stopped, and the pain in his stomach gave way to the rapid beating of his heart. The summer air turned icy cold.

It was *she*.

It was Amélie's grave.

She had been dead for the past six months.

He now remembered her reference to an undisclosed illness; how thin she looked when he saw her for the final time.

Then that question in her letter: *Who can say how much time we have?*

He had thought she was referring to him, sounding a note of caution about his age.

In fact, she had been talking about herself.

~

Berlioz stayed indoors for a week, thinking about the episodes of love in his life.

Each had been remarked upon in his work – excepting this one. There would be no memorial in music to Amélie. He had put down his pen for good. This time he would treat a tragic death as a call to action, instead of reflection.

Most of the great loves in his life had been snatched away. Only one remained that was in need of resolution – perhaps a happy one after all this time – and she was still alive. This time he would try to fulfil the promise of a final glorious relationship that he had failed in doing with Amélie.

It would end as it had begun. He decided to pick up the thread of nearly fifty years ago and seek out his star – his Stella.

POSTSCRIPT

Berlioz tracked down the now 67-year-old Estelle Fournier and visited her in Lyon to resume their friendship. Gently rebuffing his declaration of love, she was nonetheless happy to receive him as a guest over several ensuing summers. The episode is described in the closing pages of his *Mémoires*.

Hector wrote to her almost every month up to his death in March 1869.

Estelle died in 1876.